Praise for Louise Herbert and *Rest Assured*

"In *Rest Assured* Louise Herbert offers you kind, comforting, and realistic information about meeting your baby's sleep needs and calming your anxieties. Her extensive expertise in supporting new mothers helps you to navigate sleep with a clear understanding of your baby's biological expectations and abilities, and a critical eye on the unrealistic expectations of society, so you can focus on nurturing your baby and yourself."

—Professor Helen Ball
Durham Infancy & Sleep Centre
Durham University

"Warm, reassuring, and filled with advice for how to handle (and think differently about) baby sleep, this book is ideal for any parent who wants sleep solutions that are truly responsive—and a welcome antidote to the deluge of sleep books that primarily champion forms of cry-it-out."

—Amanda Ruggeri
Journalist

"This beautiful book feels like a giant hug at a time when we need it most. With so much conflicting information out there, Louise's words truly are a gift. Every page is so comforting and helps us feel guided, held, and supported in trusting our own instincts and connecting with our babies."

—Dr. Aoife Durcan
Author of Your Highly Sensitive Child

"*Rest Assured* is a wise and tender invitation to trust yourself, and your baby. Louise draws on lived experience, layered storytelling, and science to offer a grounded, practical, and affirming companion that helps parents feel more confident, steady, and connected to their babies, and to themselves."

—Dr. Sophie Brock
Motherhood Studies Sociologist

"As a professional, I appreciated the solid science in Louise's book. As a mom, I felt seen, reassured, and more confident in my instincts. *Rest Assured* is a compassionate and practical guide to baby sleep that belongs in the hands of every parent and professional who supports families."

—Jessica Guy, PhD

Rest Assured

THE *HEART* AND *SCIENCE* OF
NURTURING BABY SLEEP

BY
LOUISE HERBERT

JB JOSSEY-BASS™
A Wiley Brand

Published by John Wiley & Sons, Inc., Hoboken, New Jersey.
Published simultaneously in Canada.

ISBNs: 9781394312023 (Paperback), 9781394312047 (ePDF), 9781394312030 (epub)

For general information on our other products and services or for technical support, please contact our Customer Care Department within the United States at (800) 762-2974, outside the United States at (317) 572-3993 or fax (317) 572-4002.

Wiley also publishes its books in a variety of electronic formats. Some content that appears in print may not be available in electronic formats. For more information about Wiley products, visit our web site at www.wiley.com.

Library of Congress Control Number: 2025042631 (print)

Cover Design: Jon Boylan
Cover Images: © Taawon/stock.adobe.com, © Chinnapong/stock.adobe.com
Author Photo by Holly Osborne

Printed and bound by CPI Group (UK) Ltd, Croydon, CR0 4YY

C9781394312023_281125

For my babies, always.
And for all of our great, great, great grandbabies.

Contents

Foreword by Dr. Vanessa LaPointe

I remember so viscerally the experience of being chided—even while still pregnant with my first child 22 years ago—about how I shouldn't let him "rely" on me for sleep. My job so to speak, in the estimation of pretty much anyone I talked to, was to make him learn how to self-soothe lest he never figure it out. There were all sorts of specifics that came with this unsolicited advice (aka judgment): you need to get him out of your room by nine weeks. . .if he isn't sleeping through by six weeks, you need to sleep train. . .you aren't a human pacifier, so don't let him use you like one. . .and so on. The voices were loud and incessant. Some of them were family, some of them were friends, some of them were professionals, and some of them were absolute random strangers in the supermarket line-up. It seems sleep business is everybody's business.

Now, keep in mind I already had one graduate degree in the field of child development under my belt and a doctoral degree well underway at the time. I knew about the gorgeous dependency of human infants—exactly as nature designed. I knew about the importance of contact and closeness. I knew that my baby's trust in me was going to be foundational to everything else to come for him developmentally and otherwise. And yet, there was this horrible doubt that pushed its way into my knowing. What if they were right? What if I wasn't doing it the way I was supposed to? What if this caused problems for my child?

As the voices grew louder and more insistent, especially those closest to me, I caved. My perfect boy was closing in on 12 months and hadn't yet "slept through the night." And so, the sleep training agenda was enacted. I fed him and settled him and then laid his sweet little head down in his crib, turned my back on him, and walked out of his room, closing the door behind me. So foreign was this move to him that the cries started immediately. I remember my back sliding down his closed bedroom door as I huddled in a heap on the hallway floor, my own tears now started to roll down my face. I got sweaty, and my heart was racing. It felt like I had been there for hours when it had been only two minutes.

And then. It happened. Instinct. Knowing. Nurturing. Truth. And, I remembered who I was and who my baby was. Both organisms of attachment designed by the forces of nature to be in contact and closeness whenever, however, and for as long as was needed. I launched to my feet, tore open that door, picked up my boy, and stood strong forevermore in my conviction of what I knew he (and I) needed.

Rest Assured. As I read the words on these pages, they moved through me like a gentle breeze, cleansing and sweet. The perfect balance of informed expertise and intuitive nurturing. Having this book when my babies were little would have changed so much for me. What a gift it would have been to be released and even encouraged to lean into my natural instinct to carry and cuddle and connect around everything to do with sleep. And if that is true for me—who had nearly three degrees under my belt when I became a mom—I can't even imagine what it would be like trying to find your own *knowing* in the world of sleep, including standing up to the chiding voices, without the degrees and so-called expert status.

Rest Assured is a book that we—and our mothers and grandmothers—have been waiting for. It's a steadying guide to help parents rest in the knowing of their hearts. . .so that their babies can rest too. It shines light on the truth of who babies are and what they actually need, while allowing all the niggling guilt of over-providing to once and for all be put to rest. This is the sleep book that every new parent in the world needs to read. And, if your babies are all grown like mine, it is the sleep book that will heal your heart and cement your own knowing that you did it perfectly when you tore open that door and held them forevermore.

What our babies—and children—need is connection and, as part of that, the opportunity to be deeply dependent upon us. For it is only through the gift of deep dependence that true (not fake, not manufactured, not just a façade) independence can be arrived at. Louise says so brilliantly: "Perhaps it's not the baby's innate and appropriate expectations that are amiss here, after all. Perhaps it's the expectations of a society obsessed with independence, the earlier the better, without truly understanding how independence comes into being." And that right there is why this book stands poised to change the world.

More than a brilliant and caring reveal of how infant sleep is meant to work, this book is a call to action for caregivers everywhere to stare the world right in its eyes and say "no more." When we know better, we are called to do better. And it is my resolute belief that if just one generation of parents loved on their babies with dependence as their nurturing goal, it would change everything about how our children lived and loved and found their way forward in this thing called life.

Rest Assured. You've got this. And wherever you might find a whisper of a doubt, Louise has got you. Read on and sleep sweetly.

CHAPTER 1

Your Great, Great, Great Grandmother Didn't Sleep Train Her Babies

I don't know my great, great, great grandmother's name. I don't know where she lived, how many babies she held in her arms, nor how many she held in her heart. I honestly don't even know where she's laid to rest.

But I do know that she wasn't told to sleep train her babies. I know that she wasn't asked, over and again, whether her four-month-old was sleeping through yet. I know that she wasn't warned against feeding or rocking her children to sleep, night after night, when they were small.

How do I know all this?

Because sleep training, in any of its many disguises, hadn't yet been invented when my great, great, great grandmother was raising her babies, which means that your ancestors, too, hadn't heard the phrase, felt the pressure, or followed the expensive sleep plan.

Does this mean that our grandmothers of yesteryear spent their early years of motherhood perpetually awake? Does this mean that their babies, our more recent ancestors, were chronically sleep deprived? Does this mean that the naps and nights of times gone by were fraught, wakeful, and inherently problematic? Because this is what we're warned, isn't it? That without sleep training, we will never enjoy a moment's rest, as parents. That without setting them down and walking away at bedtime, our babies will suffer. Fail to thrive. Never learn to settle down into a peaceful, restorative, consolidated stretch of sleep at night.

The truth, and it's something that our ancestors knew but likely did not have to find the language to explain, is that no child is born with a sleep training deficit. We have survived, over thousands of years and with great success as a species, without training our youngest via disconnect, forced separation, or crying. Instead, we have evolved through nurture. Through the softness and gentleness of loving arms and midnight whispers that reassure little hearts and minds that "Mama's here." We have developed and thrived through connection and responsiveness. Our babies call for us, and we answer; our response is instinctive, like muscle memory or a calling from centuries past.

Rest assured, it's the heart and science of nurture that you'll find woven through the pages of this book, because it's nurture that our babies are born ready to receive, and which we, as parents, are sensitively, innately, and timelessly wired to offer.

■　■　■

You are a new mother, living among kin, and your camp is set up for the night.

There is a fire burning outside, and your whole family is positioned close together, beneath and within your shared nighttime shelter.

The darkness outside brings its usual sounds, and inside, your baby whimpers.

Already close, you pull him closer still, to the warmth of your body, and offer him milk.

He feeds, soothes, and sleeps.

The evening continues to darken, and the night deepens, while your baby continues to feed, soothe, and sleep until morning, his every inevitable nighttime whimper satiated without hesitation.

Among your wider group, there is a shared understanding that if those whimpers were to escalate to cries, the camp's security would become compromised.

Because with a loud or sharp cry, predators, perhaps animal, perhaps human, would be alerted to the group's whereabouts, and the risk of an ambush would be heightened.

Each and every member of the community knows this, through a mix of passed-down experience and instinct, and so you are expected to soothe your baby's whimpers without hesitation.

You can sense the group's willing:

Do not wait several minutes to test whether his hunger is real.

Do not sit a distance away to get him used to settling alone.

Do not withhold from scooping him up to get him used to existing in his own space at nighttime.

No, your group's expectation of you is to satiate your baby's hunger at his first cue.

To hold him close.

To bridge the disconnect of time and space with your arms and heartbeat and skin.

And so you feed, soothe, and settle, without considering even for a moment, that somewhere, far into the future, your bloodline will fall upon a time and world where shelters are divided into separate spaces. Where feeds are scheduled and measured. Where groups do not live in close proximity yet communal expectations still shape family practices.

While you are expected to feed, soothe, and settle, this new world will carry different expectations for new mothers. It will tell a different tale of raising babies. In this new world, the bloodline may be the same, but the story will be one of separation.

Of training.

Of independence.

And those who fall outside of these parameters will be viewed as otherly. Foolish, at best, and negligent, at worst.

■ ■ ■

If you have ever felt the pull to tend to your baby at night; to scoop your child into your arms, no matter the time of day; to offer milk, without giving any weight or thought to the idea of "bad habits," let me assure you that you are not foolish or negligent. Far, far from it, in fact. Quite simply, nurturing babies is never, ever a mistake.

Your baby is born with the same brain as a baby who was born among kin, in a shared shelter while a fire burned, thousands of years ago. Our little ones, landing here in the twenty-first century, still arrive expecting proximity and soothing, on-call.

And yet, there is a disconnect between this innate, neural expectation of our babies and the wider socially constructed, cultural expectation of our era. Today's world tends to raise its eyebrows and shake its head in disbelief at the very notion of an infant who is dependent on his caregiver for comfort and soothing after the sun has set. Yet, the expectations that our babies are born with are biological. They are in-built. We did not teach or train them. They exist just as they always have done, as a blueprint for the human experience.

And so, when we set our babies down in their cribs and they wake the second that they make contact with the mattress, instead of questioning what's wrong, perhaps we could take a moment to question, instead, what's right? What, we could ask, is biologically "expected" about this situation?

Biologically speaking, it's expected that a baby falls asleep in-arms.

Biologically speaking, it's expected that a baby will notice separation.

Biologically speaking, it's expected that a baby will soothe, settle, and sleep more easily with proximity.

Because we are carry mammals, after all. We do not hide our infants somewhere inaccessible and leave them for hours at a time, like cache mammals. Nor do we settle them in a den and return infrequently to keep them fed, like nest mammals. And we certainly do not wander while our babies try to keep up, like follow mammals. As carry mammals, we are born immature and entirely dependent, and so our infants expect and need closeness night and day.

This immaturity at birth speaks to our human need and capacity to continue gestating, postpartum. Anatomically, our large brains, and consequentially large skulls, prevent a dangerously long gestation, since the human pelvis is relatively small, and we've evolved to walk upright. Because of this, it's physiologically impossible for pregnancy to continue long enough for a human infant to exist and thrive independently immediately after birth and so we are born entirely reliant upon our caregivers, as we continue our gestation outside of the womb.

This external gestation is termed exterogestation, and it is a biologically expected feature of infancy. Because a human baby who sleeps best in-arms, who calms instantly against his mother's chest, and who cries in alarm at separation is, biologically speaking, a normal human baby.

This picture, then, of a baby waking when set down is not inherently problematic; it's biologically normal. That doesn't make it easy for us, as parents who live and breathe and function in this modern world, of course. But understanding the biological "why" is the first step in carving a path forward that works with these biological expectations, as opposed to against them, so that we can best support sleep, development, and family well-being, overall.

■ ■ ■

You are the mother of an older baby.

Your shelter is solid, with locks on the doors.

There are few rooms, and your whole family sleeps in the same space.

There are no clocks on the walls, but the moon is bright and the sky awash with stars when you and your baby rouse from sleep.

You are both alert and calm. Your baby babbles and smiles, and you notice your own thirst, so you scoop your little one up and carry him to a different space, away from your sleeping family members.

Here, you find two relatives praying and another reading by candlelight. They are not surprised to see you. Nor are you surprised to see them. You greet one another, and you quench your thirst. All the while, your baby practices his newly acquired skill of crawling and ventures across the space to retrieve a disregarded cup. He babbles to himself, happily, while your reading relative glances up from his book and smiles at your baby's play.

After a while, your baby crawls over to where you're sitting and rests his head against your lap. You scoop him up, and as expected, he leans into you and breathes deep.

Making your way back to the sleeping area, you lie down beneath a blanket and get comfortable next to your baby. He rests the back of his hand against your chest, and his heavy eyelids succumb to sleep just moments before yours follow suit. Amid the soft nighttime noises and moonlit darkness, you both sleep peacefully, together and hand-to-chest, until the sun rises, again.

■ ■ ■

In times gone by, there were no nighttime minutes illuminated on digital clock faces, asking to be counted. There was no push to track or measure the time spent awake soothing babies overnight. Nor was there shock or judgment at a child's rousing, because before the advent of clocks, nighttime was typically divided into separate "sleeps," namely, the "first sleep" and the "second sleep."[1]

Historically, sleep was understood to be biphasic in nature, occurring in two fragmented bouts overnight and separated by a relatively lengthy period of waking at some point around, or just after, midnight. This midnight pause, known as "The Watch,"[2] was once highly revered. People used it as a chance to connect, tend to the fire, and contemplate life's bigger questions during the relative quiet of the night.

Nobody would have diagnosed a wakeful baby, parent, or relative with a sleep problem for rousing, and nobody would have been unsettled or aghast at an infant's wakefulness after dark, because it was a normal feature of life. Wake ups like this were once standardized as an accepted biological norm and a nightly expectation.

Now though, with clocks and alarms and schedules that call for our full attention during a long stretch of the day, this pattern of biphasic sleep is rare, yet it's still telling to question how, and why, our sleep patterns have changed so fundamentally in just a few hundred years. The answer to this question is nuanced, but adaptability to change is a central factor, and the key change in question was the Industrial Revolution.

With the Industrial Revolution came the advent of artificial lighting, and our natural melatonin production began to alter. Melatonin, often referred to as the "sleepy hormone," helps regulate our cycling between night and day. Exposure to light suppresses the release of melatonin in the body, while exposure to darkness triggers its secretion; it's biologically normal for humans to grow sleepy at sunset, in alignment with the reduction of light. Yet, the Industrial Revolution brought new technologies, a reliance on shift work and timekeeping, and innovative lamps. So, with exposure to artificial lighting after the sun had set, a *mass adaptation* occurred.

With increased evening light exposure via artificial lighting and consequentially suppressed evening melatonin secretion, bedtimes shifted later. Yet because workers needed to rise at the same time each morning, regardless of the time that bedtime fell, the first sleep and the second sleep adapted by merging together, to ensure adequate sleep overall.

For most of us today, life's commitments are intense enough to override a split sleep sequence, and instead, we follow this modern, merged rhythm. Yet, if we listen closely enough, we might still hear of people whose biology maps to a biphasic, or even polyphasic, pattern. Especially common in older people and in babies, there are still first, second, and even third sleeps happening across the world, night after night. For some, split nights like these present a problem. For a parent expected to focus and work nine-to-five the next day, spending a couple of hours playing with a cheerful infant in the middle of the night can deepen exhaustion levels, so sleep support strategies that align with baby's biology are genuinely needed for many. Yet acknowledging this modern-day truth does not alter the biological underpinnings of a first and second sleep. And, sometimes, simply understanding the bio-normalcy of this rhythm is enough to remove the stress that's so often felt when we're awoken by a smiling and playful eight-month-old at 1 a.m.

■ ■ ■

You are a first-time mother.

You are the first mother in your family to give birth at the hospital.

Your labor is long and grueling, and after birth, your baby is placed in the hospital nursery so that you can rest.

There is a new milk available, designed especially for infants, and you are advised that this formulated infant milk is scientifically proven to be better for your baby than your own.

You are instructed to feed your baby at certain times of the day, without deviating from this set frequency, and to schedule sleep, too. You also receive a pamphlet, which discourages you from holding your baby too much, for fear of spoiling him. The printed paragraphs instruct you to set him in his crib and tend to him only in the morning, because "good babies" sleep through the night without disrupting their parents.

At home with your baby, nights are hard.

He will not soothe and settle in his crib, and you find yourself anxiously venturing to the nursery to tend to his cries throughout the night, despite the guidance you've been given.

You feel like you're failing.

You question whether your baby is somehow broken, and you wonder whether the two of you are the only pair waking through the night, instead of sleeping.

You are tired, and depleted, and your baby's cries feel like your own. On some nights, they are.

Your mother dotes on her grandbaby during the day, and you tell her that everything is as it should be. You're fine.

But she sees through your words.

Her heart, and the collective hearts of generations past, break just a little at the despair in your eyes.

Her experience had been different, but who is she to speak above the hospital staff and pamphlets?

They know best, she agrees with a smile.

But you see through her words, too.

■ ■ ■

There is not just one point in history in which our practices changed, but many.

From the rudimentary mattresses of eras past, stuffed with grasses and reeds, and laid onto the ground amid community, to the luxury organic latex mattresses of today, set upon oak bedframes in separated, quiet and secure spaces. Both our practices and our relationship with sleep have changed immensely.

Indeed, everything changes. Everything, that is, except for a baby's biological wiring toward proximity, connection, and closeness.

Because our large-brained, entirely dependent, still-gestating infants are born needing frequent calories, day and night. They're born needing to synchronize their biological functions with their caregivers, through closeness, first and foremost. They're born primed to rouse throughout the night, on multiple occasions. Not because they are somehow broken or unique in their neediness. But rather, to keep them safe, physiologically speaking, so that their external gestation, or exterogestation, can continue on as nature intended.

So, when a pamphlet puts a blocker between an infant and his nighttime milk, it makes sense that distress will follow. It makes sense that settling will be more difficult without the milk. It makes sense that baby will seek regulation via the safety and security of warm arms and a familiar heartbeat, as opposed to the shine of a polished timber crib, set within a beautifully decorated nursery.

Because our babies are born into this world with the same biological expectations as those born in eras past, and when they wake for calories and comfort throughout the night, they are still "good" babies. They are, in fact, normal babies doing normal baby things.

Of course, change, in and of itself, is not a bad thing. In fact, there is much to be thankful for and appreciative of. Yet, to support sleep safely, and with health front-and-center, looking back can guide our route forward.

There are many instances where what's deemed problematic through a modern lens, wouldn't even have been worth a mention, several generations prior. Where "I'm fine" would have been a fact, rather than an omission. Where knowing best came from within, instead of a pamphlet.

■　■　■

You are a new mother.

Your baby rests in your arms, while children of various ages play together, close by.

The room is small, and the air is filled with women's voices.

Food is being prepared, but your hands are dry and clean. You sit and nurse your baby, while the women continue their work.

A warm broth is brought to you, delivered by hands you have known since your girlhood. Hands that you trust to care for you, while you care for your child.

The voices rise and fall softly, just as they always have, and you think back to being a child, playing with your brothers, sisters, and cousins, close by to your mother and aunts and grandmother in this very room.

The same words ripple through the air, but now, you understand them. You understand this mother tongue, because you've crossed the threshold into motherhood, too.

Yet, you have not been surprised with this transition to your new role, not once. You knew what to expect because of moments like this. Moments where knowing hands brought warming broths to the newest mothers who sat nursing their babies.

You knew what to expect because of the care that's always filled the room, especially in seasons of birthing and being birthed anew.

You knew what to expect because of the wisdom that familiar conversations have brought time and again, piece by piece and word by word, as you absorbed just enough for the transition to feel known.

And so, you breathe deep and rest. Not just physically, but mentally, emotionally, and spiritually, too. Your whole being sinks deeper into the cushioning of where you sit, and you allow the familiar hum of women's words to wrap you up, cocooned until you're strong enough to add your own words to the song.

■ ■ ■

This is how it's always been. This handing down of wisdom. This cocooning and caregiving.

Only, somewhere along the way, our cocooning became more sporadic.

A brief visit here.

A phone conversation there.

Perhaps a gift, or perhaps not.

And all the while, we find ourselves transitioning to this brand-new role of motherhood without familiar hands delivering us warming broth.

Perhaps though, at its core, it's the lineage of words that we're missing even more than the broth itself.

The kitchen chatter that once shaped childhoods held a power rarely matched, because without a narrative on which to draw from, we are almost entirely unprepared for what's to come, what to expect, and what "normal" looks or feels like in this newly postpartum world.

"I'm fine" becomes our mantra, as we harden to survive.

"I'm fine" becomes our go-to answer, as we brace to avoid losing ourselves entirely.

"I'm fine, I'm fine, I'm fine," we breathe.

Over and again until we are convinced that fine-ness is all that's ever been and all we might expect.

But within us, somewhere deep, there is a longing for familiar hands, warm broth, and a cocoon of nurture that connects us to our great, great, great grandmothers, and beyond.

And if there's one thing on this earth that will pull that longing from the depths of us, it's the child who's been resting in our arms this whole entire time.

Because our babies hold the answers that we are so often seeking.

I sometimes wonder what it must have been like for my great, great, great grandmother to have held her first baby in her arms. Was she jolted into motherhood, or was her landing a little softer? Did she feel like she was failing when her baby roused for milk and soothing after dark, or did she meet those needs with a tired-yet-content inner knowing that all was just as it needed to be? Difficult at times, of course. But without alarm or a push for training.

Because human biology cannot simply be trained away.

In the 1990s, researcher Thomas Wehr[3] set out to prove that human sleep could be unconsolidated and polyphasic. In his study, artificial lighting was removed from a group of participants for 14 hours each day, allowing for just 10 hours of light exposure. The group, who usually slept in one continuous stretch throughout the night, altered their sleep patterns after just *four weeks* of these artificially controlled 10-hour days. After these four weeks, *every participant* had transitioned away from a singular, consolidated stretch of sleep overnight, to a polyphasic pattern, typically segmented into two bouts, and broken by a period of wakefulness lasting from between one and three hours.

The take-home message? It took four weeks to "undo" hundreds of years of technological advancement and human adaptation.

What's striking here, though, is the overlap between this study and the social drive toward sleep training babies. Because we are told, over and over, that we *must* train our babies to sleep independently and for long stretches overnight. We are informed, time and again, that this training requires disconnect and is an integral rite of passage for every infant. Yet, what's rarely mentioned, but seen over and over, time and again, are babies who supposedly "require" training on repeat. These are the families who grow ever more distressed when what they believed to be progress is suddenly lost to a development leap, a cold, or a busy day.

This "undoing" of our modern patterns of behavior rings true in both Wehr's sleep study and in the homes of repeatedly sleep-trained infants. Because even though we may adapt to our environment, our biology sets our baseline. We are wired and driven to exist in synchrony with light cycles and seasons, and even with training or adaptation, we are still primed for this biological "remembering."

When we gaze at our babies' chubby cheeks, their dimpled hands and larger-than-life eyes, I am certain that there are pieces of us that are wired to remember, too.

Our biology remembers what our bloodline knew, in the years before our shelters were secured, our nights consolidated and our entry to motherhood sanitized. Biologically, we are set to remember what our ancestors knew, long before we were told to set our babies down and walk away. On a cellular level, we are primed to remember what our great, great, great grandmothers knew, long before we ever heard the words "good" and "baby" being linked together as a standard to train.

■　■　■

You are sitting in your rocking chair at 2 a.m.

Your baby is sleeping in your arms, but you dare not set him down in his crib.

The room is mostly dark, with a slight orange glow coming from the night-lamp, and a too-bright glare coming from your phone screen every time you check the time.

Your mind dances between two extremes.

You wonder if you're doing it wrong. If you were cut out for this role. If you're the only mother wide awake and rocking at 2 a.m.

Yet the sight and feel of your baby in your arms feels like a balm to those thoughts.

He woke for milk, and that's okay. He's so small, still.
He needs my arms, and that's okay. I'm his safe space.
He settles best when I'm right here, and that's okay. Together, we're
a perfect team.

When you take just a moment to pause and breathe through the stillness, you notice the peace that fills the room.

A car drives by outside, disturbing the peace just a little, and you lift an arm to part the drapes and peek outside. Across the street, a fair way in the distance, you notice another light flicker.

Another mother.

How could you know? You cannot, and yet, you are certain.

You're not the only one.

Allowing the drapes to fall, you stand, baby in arms, and softly pace the room before stalling at the crib.

You lower your baby, and of course, he notices the cool air whoosh past as he's set down. You whisper into the darkness, "Mama's here," and hover over his crib, your warm hand on his belly until he settles.

He will wake again at 4 a.m.

How could you know? You cannot, and yet, you are certain.

Only, this knowing feels less like knowing and more like remembering.

You retrieve your hand. You could return to your bed. But you don't. Instead, you linger a moment, or maybe more. You linger just to gaze at this being who seems so brand new, yet carries the blood and knowing and remembering of so many before.

And so, there you stay, just for now.

Two figures in the night, but never the only ones.

■ ■ ■

Pause

"Our babies hold the answers."

In the early years of parenting, it can help to reframe our babies' behaviors through a biologically normal lens.

Doing so won't change the era we live in or the cultural expectations we navigate daily, but it can relieve some of the pressures that arise when our babies rely on us wholeheartedly at sleep times, wake to feed throughout the night, or follow their own rhythms instead of a set schedule.

Because it can be deeply stressful to believe that we've somehow caused this dependency, whether by avoiding sleep training, following "ineffective" routines, or offering comfort at bedtime. And yet, this is exactly the message new parents are confronted with: that if our infants don't settle and sleep through the night, independently, we are to blame.

So, let's pause for a moment.

Woven throughout this book, you'll find space to pause and reflect so that we can reframe the narrative around infant sleep to one that makes biological sense and centers *nurture.*

Each *Pause* section includes prompts and support suggestions designed to encourage reflection and equip you with tools to bring more ease, peace, and healthier sleep to this season of raising babies and young children.

Because sometimes, simply taking a moment to pause and reflect can bring clarity, awaken an inner knowing, or even spark a *remembering*, helping us find steadiness in this wonder-filled, yet-tiring, chapter of life.

■ ■ ■

"My baby will only settle in my arms."

Your baby's answer: "I'm brand new, mama. Your heartbeat is my most familiar sound, except for your voice. It's cold out here, on the outside of your skin, but when I'm close to you, I can breathe deeply and settle in. When you hold me, I can feel my body relaxing and my eyelids beginning to close. I feel safe, mama, right here cuddled close, with the thud of your heart lulling me to sleep. I know it can feel like a lot, but it won't always be like this. One day, I'll settle without this closeness, I promise, but for now, your arms feel like home."

Prompt: How do you feel when your baby falls asleep in your arms?

Rest Assured, a Nurturing Approach

Falling asleep in-arms is often labelled as a "fail" for parents, while having a baby who falls asleep *drowsy but awake* in their own sleep space is considered a "win."

From a biological viewpoint, falling asleep with closeness and proximity is not an exception; it's the norm. Holding our little ones close isn't a problem to fix; in fact, it's one of the surest ways to support a baby to sleep.

Why? Because *closeness fuels development.*

Closeness supports the rapid growth and "wiring" of the infant brain that occurs during the first years of life. Our babies don't just crave contact; they need it to regulate. In the realest terms, we *share our calm* with our babies; they "borrow" our calm and our nervous systems to support and regulate their own.

This is because regulation is a cornerstone of healthy sleep. Humans of all ages struggle to sleep well when stress is high or acute, and babies are no different. When we hold them close, we down-regulate their stress response, supporting their sleep overall.

We can think of the interplay between caregiver and child as an interconnected dance, best supported through:

- Closeness, especially skin-to-skin contact
- Attunement, tuning into baby's unique cues
- Responsiveness, trusting and responding to baby's unique needs as they arise

That said, supporting regulation doesn't mean holding baby 24 hours a day, 7 days a week. Independent sleep can often bring a sense of relief for us, as parents, and thankfully, a nurturing approach to crib sleep doesn't necessitate training or forced separation. Instead, it ensures that the transition feels safe, gradual, and connected.

(continued)

Supporting Crib Transfers

Crib transfers are a hot topic in the infant sleep world, with many approaches focusing on "teaching" babies via disconnect, but a nurturing approach differs.

This transition is best supported by reducing stress, not increasing it. Rather than the crib feeling like a replacement for a parent's arms, we can help baby associate it with comfort and security.

We want to down-regulate baby's stress response, not activate it, so we can begin this transition gradually and gently. Instead of aiming for setting little ones down "drowsy but awake," we can ease them into their crib when they are already in a deep, relaxed sleep. This might involve waiting for 10 minutes or so after baby has fallen asleep before making the transfer.

Signs of a deep sleep include:

♦ Relaxed hands (no longer clenched fists)
♦ Loose, floppy arms
♦ Slow, even breathing

Using the "Three-Point Touchdown" Technique

To help prevent baby's Moro reflex (startle reflex) from triggering, we can use the Three-Point Touchdown when setting baby down:

1. First, lower baby's feet onto the mattress.
2. Then, gently lower their bottom.
3. Finally, ease their back down.

This gradual contact signals safety to baby's nervous system, helping them settle and sleep in their crib.

The result? A well-settled baby, peacefully asleep in their sleep space, even (and especially) after having been soothed, rocked, or comforted to sleep in-arms.

CHAPTER 2

It Feels Hard Because It Is Hard

It's 10.30 a.m. and your baby hasn't napped yet.

She woke as usual, just after 6 a.m., and drank her milk before eating a little oatmeal.

After playtime on the mat, you read a story together until your phone pinged to let you know that it was nap time.

And so, you made up a bottle, zipped your little one into her sleeping bag, and settled down in the rocking chair, as you always do.

Only, nap time did not happen.

Your baby drank her milk, but she did not fall asleep.

She twisted her body within her sleeping bag, instead of settling into the cozy fabric, as she does on any other day.

She pushed away from your arms, instead of sinking into you.

She grew fussy and steadily louder, instead of calming and quieting.

So, you ditched the rocking chair and the sleeping bag alongside any remaining hope of a nap and made your way back to the scattered books on the playmat, where the clock on the wall shows that it's now half past 10, an hour after this morning's nap was planned.

Your chest feels tight with a mix of irritation and frustration. Morning nap is your time, as much as it is your baby's. A chance to get a head start on the day, hands-free, before you're back to holding and soothing and feeding and changing diapers again.

You notice the pile of laundry left close to the sofa. Your mind runs through the groceries that need ordering and the breakfast

17

bowls in the sink. Your irritation deepens, cut only with the guilt that co-exists alongside your need for a little time for yourself.

Do other mothers crave space like this?

Do other mothers feel the loss of a missed nap quite so acutely?

Do other mothers have helpers or extra hours in the day to get everything done?

You wonder if you're cut out for this, as your playful, brilliant girl sits close by, chewing at the edge of a Cinderella board book in a triumphant bid farewell to nap time.

■ ■ ■

When we were young, we were told fairytales.

Fairytales of beautiful princesses, existing on pedestals, in faraway castles and towers.

When we were young, we were told stories.

Stories of rescues and fairy godmothers and happily ever afters.

Now, our princess gowns are grubby with milk and oatmeal, yet our faraway towers remain steadfast.

"I've been feeling lonely," a mom semi-whispers to me from across the screen.

"It's weird, I know. I feel lonely, but I'm never actually alone." Her words are the same words as every one of us who's ever felt isolated navigating long days with young babies.

We rise in the morning, after a wakeful night, and prepare breakfast. We read stories, change diapers, and chase naps. Our minds and hours are filled with the work that once would have been shared. We try to hold it all together, tick all the boxes, and smile in all the right places.

But it feels hard.

It feels hard to exist in a baby bubble, where adult conversations are far and few between. It feels hard to juggle the day-to-day demands of life, with a baby in arms almost constantly. It feels hard to watch a nap slip away, when that hour had been hope-filled and ringfenced as an hour to exist and breathe, hands free.

"I have a schedule and a step-by-step routine," the mom from across the screen tells me, "It helps me feel more in control, even if it's just the two of us, day after day."

A schedule and a step-by-step routine.

A little order can feel like balm.

"Only," she pauses, "When things fall off track, I feel like I'm losing my damn mind."

And this is where so many of us find ourselves: making the first-hand discovery that in this season where we perch high upon clifftops within iron-clad towers, control is merely an illusion.

Once upon a time, the daily grind would have been divided between several capable hands, and the isolation of new parenthood would have been inconceivable. This is because, in times gone by, living solo or in small units would have been risky; there was safety in numbers, alongside common sense. More hands meant easily divided labor, yet naps still wouldn't have been pinned down.

Instead, babies would have slept against the chests and backs of their mothers and aunts. Wrapped in cloth and carried wherever the day took them, their sleep needs would have been met without planning or scheduling.

Now, one of the most frequent questions that new parents ask is, *what's the best nap schedule for a six-month-old? Or for an eight-month-old? Or for a one-year-old?*

We have been told that there is an "answer." We've been assured that there is a "best" amid worse options, which we must seek out and implement, or else. We are, in fact, awash with information that tells us, categorically, that there is such a thing as "the perfect nap."

The perfect nap is two hours in length, they tell us, and occurs independently, in a crib, in a darkened nursery. The perfect nap, they are sure, begins at a set time of the day, and counts only if we set baby down "drowsy but awake" and walk away. There is no space for contact napping when aiming for perfection. In fact, it is only through the successful implementation of the perfect nap that our babies can be awarded the title of "good napper" and, by default, that we can rest easy in the knowledge that we are managing sleep correctly, as "good parents" atop our pristine pedestals.

The perfect nap offers a sense of illusion that's hard to resist. It's a chariot, a glass slipper, a happily ever after. Yet chasing this fairytale nap often leaves us held against our will, tower-bound, feeling like the only parent whose slipper simply doesn't fit.

Because the perfect nap, in all of its fairytale glory, simply doesn't exist. Or, it doesn't exist as we are led to believe it does.

The truth is, today's perfect nap will look different to tomorrow's. And your baby's perfect nap will look different to my baby's perfect nap, which will look different from our friend's baby's perfect nap, and so on.

Perhaps your baby has never napped for longer than half an hour at a time. The myth of the perfect nap would have us believe that this scenario is a problem in need of a fix, yet biology tells us that this is a norm of infancy. During the day, as humans, we're wired for wakefulness. Our circadian rhythm dictates that we feel sleepier at night, driven by increased levels of melatonin, yet babies are growing fast—in both body and brain—which means that they genuinely cannot maintain wakefulness for very long periods of time.

Naps serve a fundamental purpose in these early years; they segment the day into manageable periods of wakefulness, occurring when tiredness peaks and lasting long enough to relieve the sleep pressure that's been building. When we consider the biological predisposition for babies to spend their days playing (learning) and practicing their newfound skills (consolidation and integration of learning), shorter naps are easily explainable.

Alternatively, perhaps your baby sleeps for long stretches during the day, but only in your arms. Again, the myth of the perfect nap tells us that this scenario is problematic, since "the perfect nap" is supposedly independent. Yet when we consider an infant's predisposition for closeness, it becomes clear that napping in the arms of a nurturing caregiver is fully explainable via a biological lens, too. Because when we hold our babies close, their physiology "maps" to ours. We term this phenomenon co-regulation, and it occurs on a cellular level.

My temperature regulates my baby's temperature.

My heartbeat regulates my baby's heartbeat.

My breathing regulates my baby's breathing.

It is through regulation that our human physiology can rest and digest, and our nervous systems can activate in such a way that cues biological safety. We are not in a state of alarm when we are regulated, so our energy stores can be used for growth and repair, as opposed to threat management.

At every age, proximity with a loved one acts to connect and map otherwise separate biological systems between people. We borrow each other's calm simply via closeness. It's this synchronicity that explains why many babies will nap for hours in arms yet wake just moments after being set down in a crib. Even if sleep needs have been met, the biological benefits of remaining close and calm continue to support a myriad of systems. Such closeness may not always be easy or possible to facilitate, but if and when it does occur, one thing is certain: contact napping is not biologically problematic.

We know then that some infants are natural catnappers, taking brief but frequent naps each day. Others consolidate their daytime sleep from an early age, sleeping for long stretches relatively consistently. Others, still, will sleep anywhere and everywhere, while their peers will settle only in a very specific environment. And we also know that all of this, every single piece of it, is subject to change.

"Just as I think I have it figured out, it changes again," the mom from across the screen sighs, "Even when I try to follow the exact steps I took on a good nap day!"

Many of us will be familiar with the act of chasing the perfect nap. It's so easy to believe that if only we match the timings exactly, create the exact same pre-nap routine, use the exact same sleeping bag, and sing the exact same lullaby, we'll be able to crack the nap code. Yet, there isn't a singular code to crack. The "data" we're working with changes, as do the very real demands of life outside of the naptime bubble.

It feels hard.

It's hard to tune out the idea of the perfect nap and to tune into the ever-changing being in front of us, all while being a functioning member of a society that runs by the clock.

It feels hard, because it is hard.

■ ■ ■

It's 7 p.m. and your baby isn't asleep.

You're exhausted after working all day and getting stuck in traffic on the drive back home from daycare.

At pick-up, your key worker had smiled as usual, and reassured you that your baby girl had enjoyed her day. You felt relieved that she'd had fun and grateful that she's cared for, but the words still stung.

At home, you heat up leftovers and wipe down the kitchen, baby in arms.

She won't be set down, but you don't mind. You need her close, too.

After some much-needed warm food, you play together briefly before running a bath.

Darkness hasn't yet fallen, and you make a mental note to order block out blinds for the nursery, while your daughter splashes the bath water in delight. The water rains down across the tiles.

You scoop your baby girl up, dry her off, and dress her ready for bed, but she's too wired to settle.

She nurses a little, unlatches, and babbles. Over and again, she unlatches and relatches, and your exhaustion deepens.

You wonder, silently, whether other mothers hit a wall at 7 p.m.

You wonder to yourself whether other mothers feel quite so touched-out and overstimulated by the time bedtime rolls around.

You wonder, in your head, whether other mothers are sat latching and unlatching as the evening slips away.

The clock on the wall ticks closer to 8 p.m. and your patience is a puddle on the floor. You silently calculate the minutes of sleep lost to this bedtime latching marathon. Your eyes fill with tears, but you blink them away. You're relieved to be home and grateful to be holding your baby girl in your arms after a long day, but the tears still sting.

■   ■   ■

We are told that "7 'til 7" is the ideal.

We are told that anything that differs from this regular pattern of tucking our little ones into bed at 7 p.m. and scooping them back up again 12 hours later is a problem to fix.

Yet, babies don't often fit within these parameters.

Some babies are born with naturally higher, or lower, sleep needs than their counterparts, while others are born with a biological drive to be more, or less, active during the evening than their peers. This internal, biological predisposition toward a specific optimal time of functioning during the day is referred to as a person's *chronotype*, and the difference between "morning people" and "evening people" has been long accepted and woven into our cultural understanding via terms such as "early bird" or "night owl," respectively.

What this means, in practical terms, is that there is no one-size-fits-all, "correct" bedtime that all babies and young children must adhere to in order to get enough rest and to thrive. In fact, there are many cultures across the world in which 7 p.m. would be considered very, very early for children (of any age) to be tucked into bed.

There are also seasonal differences to consider, alongside these cultural and geographical differences. For locations with seasonal variability, a 7 p.m. bedtime might feel reasonable in the dark, cold depths of winter but wholly unrealistic during the long, bright evenings of summer. Why? Because babies, just like adults, are more prone to fall asleep later in the evening during the summer than they are during the winter, simply because of the external environmental cues of daylight and, often, more outside noises, too. That is, a 7 p.m. bedtime during the winter months, when it's already dark and mostly quiet, is likely to be easier to facilitate than a 7 p.m. bedtime during the height of summer, when the sun is still shining, the birds still singing, and there's a garden party in full swing across the street.

Yet, our external world also carries a contradiction. While nature may be sending biological signals to allow for long, slow summer evenings, our day-to-day expectations and rhythms tend to be relatively unwavering, no matter the season we're in. This means that the alarm will still wake us at 6 a.m., no matter how early or late we went to bed, and our shift will still start at 9 a.m., no matter how long baby spent latched the night before.

How many of us have found ourselves watching the clock tick steadily later as we rock or feed or soothe our babies to sleep, counting backward from a set wake-up time and feeling ever more discouraged as the window for sleep reduces minute by minute?

How many of us are familiar with the inner contradiction of wanting to spend as much time as possible reconnecting with our little ones after a day spent apart, while also needing—truly needing—a little time and space to decompress in the evening?

How many of us blink through tears of frustration or overwhelm during bedtime, and chase them back with a shot of guilt for having the audacity to hold resentment for something that's apparently supposed to come so easily?

It feels hard.

This work of raising babies is not as easy as the fairytales would have us believe, and from one mother to another, it's not audacious to resent a long, fraught, or latched bedtime.

Just as it's not audacious for a baby to take a while to fall asleep, to resist bedtime when those external cues are signaling wakefulness, or to seek connection after a period of separation.

"Bedtime is my worst time of day," is a statement that I hear often. And it's a statement that is always, without exception, accompanied by guilt. We are taught to expect and create a picture-perfect routine, after all. To tuck our little ones into bed, read a story out loud, and whisper goodnight with a kiss. Because we were not raised with tales of princesses juggling perma-latched infants or lying in the dark beside restless toddlers while the evening slips steadily by.

As parents, we often find ourselves juggling several variables all at once. We're tasked with balancing our baby's unique sleep needs and chronotype, with the external cues of the evening, all while maintaining a steady level of functionality as contributing members of wider society. We need to pay the bills, show up to our commitments, and simultaneously flex and weave with the ever-changing needs of the child in front of us.

This juggling is not easy.

In fact, it feels hard.

And it feels hard, because it is hard.

■ ■ ■

It's 1 p.m. and you're late to lunch.

Your baby napped later than usual, but you didn't want to cut nap time short, as she was tired after a wakeful night.

You leave the house as soon as she wakes and drive the 20 minutes to meet your friends and family.

It's been a while since they've seen your baby—since she was brand new, in fact—and there are many comments about how much she's grown and how much she looks like her daddy.

"Her nap overran?" They ask, eyebrows raised.

"Did she not sleep well last night?" They ponder.

"Are you not sleeping through yet?" They ask her directly.

Your baby stares through their questions and they laugh, "So serious!"

You smile, while your brain races.

"Let me just tell you," the questions turn to directions, "You need to get that girl on a schedule!"

You smile, while your heart sinks.

"You can't have her running the show! Your cousin Becky's neighbor's baby is like clockwork: three naps a day and sleeping through the night!"

You smile, while your feet want to run.

But they don't, of course, because you have glass slippers to keep shiny and new.

■ ■ ■

We are told that comparison is the thief of joy, yet we are primed to compare, as humans.

We often look outside of ourselves for experience, when we're seeking knowledge. We look for guidance when we need direction. We look for answers when we have questions.

Using what we hunt and gather from those around us, we then cross-compare and assess our own reality against the benchmark that we've collected.

Clinically and across sectors, such comparisons help create frameworks and screening protocols to identify issues and offer early interventions. At its best, comparison saves and improves the quality of lives.

Yet, there are inherent issues and complexities that also arise in any scenario of comparison, and the main one, perhaps, is how do we know—truly, absolutely know—that the external marker we are standardizing and comparing our reality to, is the benchmark that will serve us best?

When it comes to raising babies, it's natural for new parents to look outside of ourselves and to compare and contrast with other, more seasoned parents, when seeking knowledge, guidance, and answers. In years gone by, we would have been surrounded by a small and trusted community that existed within the same reality. The group would have shared activities, daily rhythms, and communal goals, and it's likely that guidance from group members would have felt like well-fitting parameters to work within, while the unique cues and needs of each new baby would have filled in the detailed middle.

Indeed, we're told that it takes a village to raise a child, and when that village is close in physical proximity and shares the same ideologies and daily grind, it becomes easier to imagine an external comparison, benchmarking, and sense of steering as being supportive for new parents, raising babies among kin.

Now, our villages are disbanded, both physically and ideologically. We live different lives to our neighbors, to our friends interstate, and to our family overseas. Even our goals and expectations in life are individualized, as opposed to shared. And with this societal rooting in independence as opposed to interdependence, the human act of comparison has developed a tendency to make life harder, not easier.

Because external, generic benchmarks are unlikely to make sense to the unique circumstances and goals of mother–baby dyads living a life far away from the proverbial village.

If I work shifts, I cannot benchmark my daily rhythm to my friend who works from home.

If I breastfeed my baby, I cannot benchmark her nighttime feeding needs to my formula-fed niece's nights.

If I follow my baby's lead when it comes to sleep, I cannot benchmark the timing of her naps to a generic sleep schedule.

Without this sense of solidarity and shared benchmarking, it's easy to feel like the only one, like the only mother doing it this way. The only mother chasing naps. The only mother resenting bedtime. The only mother without a solid schedule or the ability to plan and attend a lunch out.

"I don't know what I'm doing wrong." These are words I hear over and again, as we try to fit in with external expectations and repeatedly fall short.

"My baby didn't get the sleep memo." This is how it feels, for many of us, as a nap overruns and we arrive late to a catch-up, yet again.

We are told that we must bounce back after having a baby. We are expected to fit right back into life as it was and to show up unchanged for work meetings and family lunches. And our babies are expected to fit in, too: to follow our schedules and coo and smile in all the right places, just like Mom.

This is the benchmark that society offers us, and when we fail to meet it—or perhaps, when we don't want to—we are tower-bound once again.

It feels hard.

It feels hard to be an outsider, looking in. It feels hard to juggle competing needs while fielding opinions or questions. It feels hard, and even a little rebellious, to trust our own babies' rhythms instead of the rhythms of our cousin's neighbor's babies'.

"I'm the only one who's doing it this way." This is how it feels when we're walking on glass and balancing precariously between two worlds; the world of the life we knew before, where our friends and families are still firmly rooted, and this new world, where our focal point is the child that we're carrying.

It feels hard to bridge two worlds. And it feels hard, because it is hard, not because we're doing it wrong.

■ ■ ■

You unlock your front door and step inside with a sigh of relief.

Your baby fell asleep five minutes from home, after fighting sleep all day, and you know this spells disaster for an early bedtime, but you're too tired to care.

It feels hard.

Inside, you set the car seat down and scoop your sleeping baby into your arms.

You could attempt to set her down in her crib, but the transfer from car seat to crib is infamously treacherous, so instead you decide to let your daughter sleep in your arms while you take a minute to relax.

You scroll on your phone, while your baby girl dozes against your chest, and you see images of pastel nurseries, beige onesies, and perfect smiles.

You read about perfect family units, taking perfect day trips, with perfectly scheduled two-hour naps.

You cannot help but compare.

Your baby opens her eyes, just for a moment, as if to check that you're there.

"Mama's here," you whisper, instinctively, and your baby sighs her big sigh before closing her eyes again. Just right.

You notice, for the first time all day, the knot in your stomach beginning to loosen.

You feel your own chest rise and fall, slow and steady, and even though the day wasn't pastel or beige or always smiling, right now feels just right.

It feels imperfectly perfect.

It feels like a remembering.

You shuffle a little and sink into the sofa to get comfortable.

You might be here a while, but that's okay.

You notice something rigid digging into your back, and you carefully lean to the side to dislodge a princess figurine that's been lost down the back of the sofa for goodness knows how long.

You hold the figurine in your hands and notice her smiling, vacant face staring back at you, before tossing her into the toy box with the plastic fairies and plush kittens.

Your baby smiles in her sleep, and you notice her cheeks dimple.

She fits perfectly in your arms, and even after a hectic day, and even without the pastel backdrop, you find yourself smiling too.

It's not easy, you know.

But right now, it feels just right.

■　■　■

Pause

"My baby doesn't follow a sleep schedule."

Your baby's answer: "I'm learning a lot, mama. My brain is growing quickly, and I'm changing every day. As I change, my sleep alters a little, too. Some days, I will nap longer than other days. Some nights, bedtime will be much easier and faster than other nights. Thank you for noticing when I'm tired and for letting me play when I'm not. Thank you for soothing me after a busy day, even when you're tired too. Thank you for trusting my needs and rhythms, as I grow and change so much."

Prompt: How do you feel when your baby's sleep needs differ from a generic sleep schedule?

Rest Assured, a Nurturing Approach

All babies enter this world with differing and ever-changing sleep needs. This means that a schedule that works for one baby won't necessarily work for another baby of the same age. In addition to this natural variation, sleep needs fluctuate with development, illness, or even the level of stimulation a child experiences prior to sleep.

With this in mind, we all have our own unique sleep profile, and babies are no different. Many parents ask how many hours their baby *should* be napping or how many hours of sleep their little one *should* be getting overnight, yet there is no pinpoint accurate, one-size-fits-all answer to these questions. Some babies will naturally have lower or higher sleep needs than their peers.

Even the National Sleep Foundation[4] recognizes this variation across individuals. Their published sleep ranges indicate that a difference of up to eight hours can still be considered appropriate between individual babies.

Similarly, there is no "ideal" nap schedule, nor is there an "ideal" nap duration or location. All naps count, whether they happen in the stroller, in arms, or in the crib, and whether they last 2 hours or just 20 minutes.

(*continued*)

Naps function to take the edge off accumulating sleep pressure so that baby can continue through the day with a mind and body that's regulated enough to learn, play, and explore during wakeful periods. Some infants will naturally consolidate daytime sleep into long naps, while others are born "cat nappers," with an apparent in-built "fear of missing out" on what the day has to offer. Both are completely normal from a sleep science perspective.

Understanding Nap Transitions

While individual variations are normal, we do still see general sleep patterns across age groups, particularly in relation to when babies transition between nap stages. These transitions typically occur:

- ♦ From four to three naps: Between 4 and 5 months
- ♦ From three to two naps: Between 6 and 9 months
- ♦ From two to one naps: Between 12 and 18 months
- ♦ From one nap to none: Between 18 months and 3 years

It's so important to note that these ranges are not prescriptive. If your baby is thriving and content but naps differently than this timeline, you can trust your baby's thriving.

Many parents describe the stress of trying to follow a generic sleep schedule, so a less rigid and more easeful approach can be to get curious about the rhythms that work best for the child in front of us, and to support sleep through a more flexible, tailored lens.

Practical Ways to Support Sleep (Without a Strict Schedule)

Rather than focusing on a rigid sleep schedule, it can help to view sleep across the full 24-hour day.

- If nights are very fragmented and daytime naps are long and plentiful, reducing the frequency or duration of daytime sleep can help consolidate sleep at night.
- If bedtime is delayed or feels stressful, tailoring the timing of bedtime to baby's tiredness levels, as opposed to a generic "ideal" time, can be especially helpful.
- If it feels tricky to identify your little one's unique sleep rhythm, trialing a consistent morning wake up time can help set up the day's rhythm and create more predictability. In this way, we can view morning waking as a checkpoint, and a set wake up time can create a "ripple effect" where naps and bedtime become easier to anticipate and facilitate overall.

The Three Pillars of a Flexible Sleep Approach

At the heart of this baby-specific, responsive approach are three key elements:

- **Understanding:** Tuning in and getting curious about the rhythms that work best for our little ones, even if those rhythms contradict a more generic schedule.
- **Trusting:** Believing that baby's cues and signals are real and worthy of following. Tired signs such as yawning or rubbing eyes are far more helpful than the clock on the wall when determining whether it's time to offer a nap.
- **Responding:** Once we understand and trust our children's cues, we can respond sensitively. This may look like supporting an earlier bedtime after a busy day or pushing naptime back if baby is happily engaged in play.

The Benefits of a Tailored Approach

When we understand, trust, and respond to our babies' unique sleep needs, naps and bedtime tend to become easier overall.

(continued)

- ◆ Sleep onset, or the time it takes for baby to fall asleep, is typically shorter.
- ◆ Night waking is often reduced.
- ◆ Little ones are far less likely to "fight sleep" because they are *genuinely ready* to settle down and rest when the time comes.

By letting go of rigid sleep schedules and focusing on real-time needs instead, we can create a sleep environment that feels more peaceful, more intuitive, and ultimately, more supportive of sleep overall.

CHAPTER 3

It's Not the Baby

You are sitting across from a nurse at your baby's wellness check.

"How is he sleeping?" She asks, expectantly.

"Um," you falter a little, and your baby squirms in your arms, "He wakes a few times. . .," your voice trails off.

"Still?" Her eyes search your face for an answer and her left eyebrow arches slightly, as if shocked. Fingers dance busily across the keyboard, and your insides twist at the thought of the words forming on the screen.

Later, back at home, you replay the visit over and again. You question whether you should have stretched the truth and insisted that your wakeful baby sleeps for 12 hours at a time, every night. The word "still" repeats in your head. You question whether you're missing something that everyone else has figured out already. You worry whether your little one is falling behind. You wonder whether your baby is the only one still waking, because the nurse's arched brow and dancing fingers would suggest that he is.

Your son's frustrated calls pull you from your thoughts. He is on his hands and knees, willing himself to crawl.

"It's okay," you soothe, "You'll get it!"

His eyes find yours before he folds into your lap, in surrender.

You brush his curling wisps of hair with your fingers. When did they grow so long?

"It's okay," you offer again, "It's not a race."

And thoughts of raised eyebrows and falling behind fade away, as you wonder who it is you're reassuring.

■ ■ ■

There is something disconcerting about the idea of falling behind.

We want to know, categorically, that we're on track, because being on track has typically been a sign of safety, throughout our human history. It connects us to our wider group, where following the common path and fitting in with expectations is less likely to result in conflict. It's an innate nod toward safety. Yet, in today's world, there's a disconnect between our social norms and expectations, and our biological norms and expectations.

While human biology places nighttime rousing firmly inside the "normal" category of infancy, society tells us otherwise. Tiny words like "Still" and small gestures such as a raised eyebrow can feel weighted and consuming, when in fact it is totally expected for a young child to continue to wake through the night in the early months of life.

"Still" tells us that there is a "right time" for night waking to stop. It tells us that "most" babies meet this timing and that those who fall outside of it land outside of the group. Off track. Unsafe.

But the truth is, biology isn't out of place, because it's not the baby who is off track. Human development is not a race, after all. What's really fallen off the rails are the misplaced expectations of a culture that doesn't understand the science of how or why human infants develop the way they do.

At birth, a baby's brain is around a quarter of the size of an adult brain. This is no accident or mistake; we have evolved to support the continued, external gestation of our babies, on the outside of our skin, postpartum. This involves sensitive and close caregiving. It involves carrying and holding our babies against our bodies to support the regulation of their physiology. It involves responding to their cues and needs, night and day. It involves facilitating optimal brain growth and development, even in our smallest, everyday interactions.

And this doesn't end when the newborn phase merges into babyhood or even when toddlerhood arrives. In fact, it's generally accepted that in terms of neurobiology, infancy lasts for three whole years, at least. This means your walking, talking toddler is still firmly placed within infancy from a brain development viewpoint, and this simple shift in perspective can serve to "reset" our expectations around what's "normal" for the developmental timescale that our little ones are tracking against.

These first three years are classed as a "sensitive period" of development, and they cannot be hurried. These early years are foundational for building future health and well-being, since the life experiences that occur during this sensitive window will affect the way that the human brain is "wired" in both the short-term and the long-term. Inside the brain there are neurons and synapses. Neurons are our brain cells, and synapses are the intricate neural "highways," or connections, formed between neurons. During these early years of life, the proliferation of these synapses increases the brain's size and weight, with the brain reaching 80 percent of its adult size by age three.

During this time, the brain grows in both mass and structural complexity, and is especially malleable. We call this malleability *neuroplasticity*, or the ability to form and reorganize synaptic connections in response to experiences, and it is this experience-dependent responsiveness that explains why early interactions—and nurture—are so key for building the healthiest brains. The interactions that a child has during the first three years shape the brain's structure and function, with this adaptability and plasticity dramatically reducing once neurological infancy ends.

This doesn't mean that all children will sleep and wake like brand new babies throughout their toddler years, though. Development is continuous, after all. Yet it does speak to why a nine-month-old might "still" wake to feed during the night, why a one-year-old might "still" settle best in arms, and why a two-year-old might "still" need a parent to lie close by at bedtime.

This dependency that we witness so acutely in the early years is not accidental or a sign of a problem; it is rooted in the exponential neural growth and development that's happening day and night, and is supported by responsive, attuned care. We are molding and building brains and neural pathways with every cuddle. We are nurturing our little ones' positive relationship with sleep every time we sensitively respond to a midnight wake-up. And so, when they ask if we're "still" tiptoeing across the hallway at 2 a.m., and we're met with expectant, raised eyebrows while we consider our answer, we can hold tight to the fact that it's not the baby that's amiss. It's the hurried expectations that we find ourselves wading through, as new parents, since these expectations are considerably lacking in biological grounding.

Because ours is a culture that views children as mini adults and that places independence at the top of the pedestal of expectations for babies. We are not taught about the external womb in school. The term *exterogestation* is one that few adults will ever come across in conversation. We are not equipped with the knowledge and understanding of how brains grow best and function optimally, even though mental health struggles are ever-more prevalent. Instead, we are congratulated for markers of early independence, and in turn, the general cultural drive is toward rushing development and meeting these independence milestones as quickly as possible.

"It's not a race."

These words felt like balm when my eldest was a baby, as I stood pushing her on the swing at a local playground. They were offered by a grandma pushing her granddaughter on the adjacent swing.

"There's no rush," she went on, smiling at her granddaughter, who laughed as she swung higher and higher.

"There's no prize for getting there first, so we'll take our time, won't we?"

I don't remember the context of that brief exchange. I don't remember whether we were talking about sleep, walking, language acquisition, or calculus. I only remember the relief that flooded my body.

It's not a race. And it's not the baby. It's society's misinformed push toward early independence in place of dependency and co-regulation.

Your baby is not broken or in need of a fix, but society just might be.

■ ■ ■

You're running late for work, but there's still a load of laundry to get to before you can head out the door.

With your baby on your hip, you pull warm onesies and shirts from the dryer, one by one, while your son reaches out, points at each item, and laughs.

You carry the still-warm laundry in a basket on your free hip, as you quickly make your way to the bedroom that you share. The nursery that was so diligently planned and organized during pregnancy now sits silently waiting, and as you pass it in the hallway, you contemplate, again, whether to turn the almost-empty space into an office, just for now.

The crib has been in the main bedroom since your baby was born. It is now a staple feature of the room, and you set the clean clothes down inside its trusted oak frame without a second thought, as you usually do.

Your baby laughs again as you spin around to grab a sweater, and you notice that the big bed isn't made; its covers are a mess, and there's a pillow missing on the side that your little one tends to sleep. You wonder whether your baby is giggling at the glaring difference between the sheets in disarray and the pristine sight of the world's most luxurious laundry basket, sitting proudly and perfectly made with its oak bars and organic sheets, silently waiting for the day in which its originally intended purpose might be fulfilled.

Today isn't that day, you decide, and you spin once more to the sound of your baby's giggles, just because, before the day carries you both away.

■ ■ ■

Not too long ago, a new mom was sitting across from me, her eyes fixed on her son.

"Why won't he sleep without me?"

Her gaze scanned her baby boy's face for any sign of a problem. For any hint of a probable cause for his insistent nighttime need for closeness. Yet no cause could be found.

Meanwhile, her baby peered back from his carrier, grinning a gummy smile, completely unaware of the concern being raised.

"Shouldn't he be able to sleep by himself by now?" The question hung in the air between us, searching for an answer.

"Babies sleep best when they feel safe," I replied, "And you are your baby's safe place."

I let the words land and for the first time, the mom in front of me unfixed her eyes from her son, and her gaze searched mine, instead.

Whether she was checking for truth, reassurance, or a mix of the two, I don't know. But I watched as her shoulders relaxed and she allowed herself to breathe out, finally; her out breath reminding me of the big sigh that so many babies let out just before sleep overtakes them.

You know the one?

I call it the big sigh, the deep sigh, or the sigh of safety, and it's one of our best markers of a felt sense of safety and regulation when entering sleep. It's a letting go and a giving in, all in one. It's surrender, as wakefulness gives way to sleep.

For babies, born entirely dependent and still gestating, albeit on the outside of our skin, closeness with mom creates a deep sense of safety and regulation. Physically, we see a reduction in cortisol concentrations during skin-to-skin contact, while "feel-good" hormones like oxytocin receive a boost. Heart rate variability regulates, and vagal tone increases, which helps regulate the body's key stress-response systems, including the hypothalamic–pituitary–adrenal (HPA) axis and the autonomic nervous system. In simplest terms, these are the biological mechanisms that support a baby to downregulate alarm, through the felt safety that maternal closeness provides.[5]

For many babies, the physical separation that comes with sleeping separately to mom is enough to trigger dysregulation that takes the form of "protest" or attachment-seeking behaviors. When this happens, it's easy to begin to question whether there is, in fact, something amiss with our little ones. And yet, there is nothing wrong with a baby who won't easily settle and sleep independently in their crib. It's not the baby, and really, it's not the crib either. It's simply biology; our human drive toward safety, which is automatically found via closeness.

For many families, safely sharing a sleep space with baby can positively transform nighttimes for parents and infants alike, especially for breastfeeding duos who can benefit from such close proximity with easier feeding access and support for milk supply.[6] It's also a much-utilized way to meet both infant and parental connection needs after a working day spent apart, and this speaks to why so many cribs remain empty (or perhaps filled with laundry) while parental beds welcome children in.

Yet we are often told and sold the idea that all babies should sleep separately, so we often find ourselves asking, "Why won't he sleep in his crib?!" If this feels familiar, it can help to rephrase the question to, "Why *would* he sleep in his crib?"

What would make this sleep space feel familiar?

What would make this sleep space feel soothing?

What would make this sleep space feel safe?

When we accept the biology behind a baby's drive for closeness, it becomes so much easier to work with that biological drive and support crib sleep on baby's terms.

"He slept in the crib last night!"

The mom with the searching gaze was sitting across from me again.

"Well, for most of the night, I still brought him into bed with me for a snuggle at some point before dawn," she was smiling as she spoke.

She hadn't forced it. She hadn't set him down and walked away. She hadn't left him to cry. She had, instead, supported his sense of familiarity, soothing, and safety in a space that had felt foreign before.

She had taken her time and allowed her son to experience comfort and being comforted within this new sleep space, and this involved her presence and closeness. It involved her warm hand on his belly as he drifted off to sleep. It involved her soothing words and voice, as she offered up her own calm to her baby, with just a little more distance than he had been used to, to date.

Because with safety, comes regulation. And with regulation, comes sleep.

The mom was scanning her baby's face again, as she explained how well he'd been sleeping and how she'd stopped dreading bedtime. Yet this time, she wasn't looking for a problem; she was mapping the way her son's cheeks curved, the dimple in his chin, and the softness of his brows. I watched, again, as her shoulders relaxed, and she breathed out. The sigh of safety. An inner knowing. A remembering.

Because it's not the baby, or the crib for that matter, and it never was.

■ ■ ■

"If you go to him every time he cries, he'll expect you to *always* go to him when he cries."

The intent is well-meaning, but the words land like daggers on your skin.

"Well, he's a baby. . . ."

"Mark my words! You'll be sorry! You need to teach him who's boss now, before it's too late!"

You can feel your heartbeat rising, and your palms are sweating. You pick your baby up from his stroller, where he's been napping until beginning to fuss, and hold him against your chest. You both instantly feel calmer.

You offer a smile instead of diving headfirst into a debate and quickly excuse yourself from the room. Outside, the fresh air reminds you to breathe.

"Mark my words!"

"You'll be sorry!"

"Before it's too late!"

The words ring in your ears.

Your son's chatter pulls you from your thoughts. He is babbling at his own reflection, staring back at him from the glass door you've just come through.

You smile, and he turns his face to meet yours. His eyes scan your eyes. His mouth curls in a smile at your smile. He holds your gaze as if searching for, and instantly finding, an answer.

"If you go to him every time he cries, he'll expect you to *always* go to him when he cries."

The words are on a loop inside your skull, but you realize, that's the point. That's the whole point, right there. You want your child to look toward you, not away from you when he cries, feels unsure, or is searching for an answer.

Your baby turns his head away again and resumes babbling at his own reflection. He'd found what he was looking for.

"I won't be sorry," you whisper, and you steel yourself a little, before crossing the threshold and making your way back inside.

■ ■ ■

When a baby wakes and automatically seeks comfort or connection, there's no need to panic. There's no need to worry about a future filled with constant need-meeting or a lack of independence. There's no need to utter or heed warnings about regret. Seeking comfort and connection upon waking is normal during infancy. There is nothing amiss or extraordinary taking place.

It's only relatively recently in our human history that some cultures have fixated upon the idea and goal of independence in relation to infant sleep. Innately, we are wired to meet the needs of our youngest group members when they are too immature to meet their own needs themselves. We do this with an inner knowing that such need-meeting sets the foundations for future maturity, where independence is born of dependency.

We know now that a met need dissipates. Babies are incapable of manipulation, or the forward planning required to "take us for a ride" or "wrap us around their little finger." They are not lying in their cribs at night plotting how best to summon us at their next whim. The brain functionality that allows for such mature cognition is simply not possible in the early years of life, as it relies on the development of the frontal lobes. The frontal lobes are the parts of the brain responsible for executive functions such as planning and impulse control, and maturity tends to finalize in the third decade of life, not the third month or year.[7] In neurological infancy, or baby's first three years, we can trust that every baby-led attempt to connect or elicit a response in a caregiver is grounded in a current-and-pressing need, and that each one of these needs is real.

It's normal when he wakes from a nap and calls out. Just as it's normal when he settles when responded to. There is nothing amiss here, with this sleep-specific example of a "serve and return" interaction between parent and child. In fact, such interactions are foundational neural mirroring mechanisms, whereby emotional and social well-being help shape a child's neurological development.

It's a big deal when we respond.

The child "serves" with a cue, call, or cry, and we "return" that "serve" by responding in an appropriate and sensitive way. Through countless serve-and-return interactions like this, whereby a child calls out upon waking, and a parent responds with calming words or a soothing cuddle, the neural connections within a baby's brain that are wired for connection and regulation strengthen. And it is the strongest, most utilized connections that last in the long term, while the weaker, less utilized connections are pruned away.

"Use it or lose it" is a phrase we hear over and again in the field of neurology, and it's our role, as caregivers, to strengthen the most beneficial neural pathways for our babies. Our babies are born with a deeply rooted expectation that their cues, calls, and cries will be responded to, after all, and in the early years, this responsiveness helps "map" the pathways of the brain, wiring networks of synapses via these lived experiences. The brain in this season is described as plastic; it is shapeable, and it's this plasticity that helps develop and sculpt a child's sense of self and place within the wider world.

When we respond to a cue for feeding, a call for interaction, or a cry upon waking, we are shaping the infant brain to rest within nurture. To lean on sensitive caregiving. To expect and feel worthy of love. This is no bad thing, and over time, our babies will naturally develop more autonomy and self-care abilities; they will grow to seek and find such nurture within themselves. Crucially, this inner caretaking is made possible via the external and intense caregiving experienced during the early years.

"If you go to him every time he cries, he'll expect you to *always* go to him when he cries."

He won't.

Though I dare say most of us wouldn't mind so much if he did. Instead, he will expect, subconsciously, via a brain wired toward nurture as opposed to away from it, for his needs to be met with love.

And isn't this the whole point, right there?

Perhaps it's not the baby's innate and appropriate expectations that are amiss here, after all. Perhaps it's the expectations of a society obsessed with independence, the earlier the better, without truly understanding how independence comes into being.

■ ■ ■

It's past midnight, and your baby is calling for you after waking for the second time since bedtime.

You tiptoe across the hallway and open his nursery door, which creaks as it always does before the soft glow of the night light meets you.

You rest your hand on your baby's belly to try to settle him back to sleep, but he's restless and hungry, so you scoop him up instead.

After a feed, you consider setting him back into his crib, but you know that he'll wake again before morning, and you're tired.

So instead of returning him to his crib, you carry him with you as you make your way back across the hallway.

You climb back into bed and settle down together, your body curled around your baby's. This isn't the first night that you've brought him into the big bed with you, and for a fleeting moment, you question whether you should give in so easily.

Your baby's chest rises and falls as he breathes deep and steady, and you're brought back to the present moment, which doesn't feel like giving in at all.

It feels like peace.

Your eyes are heavy, but through the darkness you hold them open a little longer, just to scan your baby's profile in the darkness. There is no hurry here. This close, you can trace every curve of his face and note every movement and sound that he makes.

There has never been anything more perfect in the world, you're sure. And with this certainly, your eyes close and sleep overtakes you, too.

■ ■ ■

Pause

"My baby won't sleep independently."

Your baby's answer: "When I wake at 2 a.m. and call for you, it's not because I don't like my crib, mama. It's because I sleep better when I'm close to you. I can rest in your safety as you curl around me and sleep, too. I wake to check on you from time to time, or to get comfy, or for a drink of milk, but I am not alarmed. I feel safe with you next to me, but one day soon, I won't need your heartbeat so close in order to settle. I'll sleep in my own bed, and I'll feel safe there, too. Thank you for showing me, over and again, that I can depend on you, until I can depend on myself."

Prompt: How do you feel when your baby seeks your connection and comfort during the night?

Rest Assured, a Nurturing Approach

For many families across the globe, a child's biological drive toward closeness is facilitated by sharing a sleep space. This is often referred to as *bed-sharing*, or more loosely, *co-sleeping*, and it remains the most longstanding sleep arrangement in human history.

In western, educated, industrialized, rich, and democratic (WEIRD) societies,[8] such as the United States, Canada, the United Kingdom, and Australia, bed-sharing is often discouraged, while crib sleeping is encouraged. This is largely because crib sleeping provides a more straightforward way to establish external safety measures, such as a flat, clear sleep surface free from pillows, loose bedding, or other potential hazards.

Parental beds in WEIRD societies often include soft mattresses, thick duvets, multiple pillows, and cushions, making them unsafe for babies to share, and advocacy for safe and separate sleep environments has played an important role in reducing sleep environment risks.

Creating a Safe Sleep Environment

When setting up a safe and separate sleep space, we can consider the following factors[9,10]:

- Maintaining a comfortable room temperature to avoid overheating
- Using light bedding or a well-fitted baby sleeping bag
- Room-sharing with a caregiver for at least the first six months, and ideally 12 months

◆ Keeping baby's face and head uncovered (no hats, bonnets, or loose blankets)
◆ Placing baby on their back, on a firm, flat surface with no gaps or edges
◆ Ensuring that the sleep surface is free from pillows, bumpers, blankets, soft toys, and other loose bedding

Considerations for Sharing a Sleep Space Safely

Many families will bed-share intentionally or unintentionally at some stage, whether for comfort, convenience, or due to a wakeful baby. For this reason, safe bed-sharing education is important for all families. The following factors[11] can be considered when setting up a shared sleep space:

◆ Ensuring baby sleeps on their back on a firm, clear sleep surface
◆ Using a firm mattress with a tightly fitted sheet
◆ Ensuring there are no gaps, edges, or drop-offs where baby could fall or become entrapped
◆ Keeping bedding well away from baby's face and ensuring the sleep space is free from all higher-risk items, such as excess bedding, pillows, or cushions
◆ Avoiding swaddling, so baby has free movement of their arms and body
◆ Dressing baby appropriately to prevent overheating
◆ Removing any dangling cords, wires, or hazards near the sleep space
◆ Tying back long hair and removing jewelry
◆ Ensuring a caregiver is present whenever baby is sleeping in the shared sleep space, and room-sharing for at least the first six months, and ideally 12 months
◆ Avoiding bed-sharing if any adult in the bed smokes, has consumed alcohol, drugs, or sedating medication, or if baby was born prematurely or at a low birth weight

(continued)

Recognizing Sleep Red Flags

While frequent wake-ups and seeking closeness are biologically normal, some irregularities, or "red flags," may suggest an underlying issue that warrants further support, such as:

- Consistently waking every hour or after every sleep cycle for a prolonged period
- Distressed or painful awakenings
- Breathing irregularities, including snoring, mouth breathing, gasping, or long pauses in breathing
- Feeding difficulties, such as:
  - Clicking sounds while feeding
  - Dribbling milk or struggling to latch
  - Maternal pain during breastfeeding
  - Poor weight gain despite regular feeds
- Physical symptoms, including:
  - Persistent congestion
  - Rashes, eczema, or digestive discomfort
  - Restlessness during sleep
- Developmental or behavioral concerns, such as:
  - Delays in reaching milestones
  - Significant changes in behavior

If any of these red flags are present, it's not a sign that baby needs sleep training or less connection. Instead, it's a cue to explore possible underlying causes, whether related to feeding, breathing, allergies, pain, or other medical considerations. For instance, if feeding challenges arise, seeking guidance from a qualified professional can help assess factors such as oral function, structural differences, or feeding efficiency, all of which may impact sleep quality.

In situations like these, the solution is not to limit closeness or train sleep through separation. The solution is to identify and address the root cause with appropriate, evidence-based support.

CHAPTER 4

You Didn't Cause Your Baby's Night Waking

Y̶ou open your eyes to the familiar calls of your baby.

The room is dark, and the numbers on the clock face begin with a 3. You breathe out, long and deep, as if in surrender. This is the third wake up of the night. 3 by 3. It would be funny if you weren't so exhausted. Your tiredness runs deep, your bones are heavy, and your eyes are still half closed.

As you make your way to your baby's crib, you question whether you're somehow at fault. You wonder whether you're doing it wrong. You begin to believe that you must have caused your baby's night waking.

You arrive crib-side and retrieve your baby, up, up and into your arms.

"Mama's here," you whisper for the third time, and your baby hungrily whimpers as she roots for milk.

A wave of something moves through you. Is it anger? Resentment? Whatever it is, it's chased down by shame.

This doesn't feel like the books said it would feel.

This isn't what you signed up for.

This waking, waking, waking, over and over and over again, is harder than you ever imagined it would be.

Your baby drinks her milk and falls back to sleep, carefree and relaxed. Your eyes are now wide open, though your bones are still heavy with exhaustion. Tears streak your cheeks, but they are not sorrowful; they are exasperated and only made worse by the fact that you're sure, certain in fact, that you're to blame for nights like this.

"Mama's sorry," you whisper through tears, but your baby doesn't hear you, because she's fast asleep.

■ ■ ■

Our babies are not miniature adults. In the same way that our youngest humans do not yet walk or talk like their fully grown counterparts, nor do they sleep like us, either.

This difference between babies and adults seems obvious, I know, but we live in a world that places adult-like expectations on baby sleep patterns, unaware or unbothered by the vast biological differences that exist between adult sleep and infant sleep.

As humans, we function diurnally; that is, we wake during the daytime and sleep during the night. Though if you've ever spent the night pacing a dark room with a wakeful baby, there's a good chance that you've questioned whether you might have birthed a "one-off" nocturnal human. (You haven't, I promise.)

This natural "programming" toward daytime waking is driven by our circadian rhythm, which is governed by a "master clock" located within our brains (in the suprachiasmatic nucleus of the hypothalamus, to be exact) and supported by additional bodily "clocks" located throughout our tissues. This master clock and these peripheral clocks follow a 24-hour cycle and synchronize via neural and hormonal signals. It's an impressive alignment, which helps coordinate the regulation of physiological functions within the body,[12] including the sleep–wake cycle, feeding, and body temperature, adjusting these processes to the 24-hour, day-to-night cycle.[13]

So, if babies and adults follow a 24-hour circadian rhythm, why do babies wake throughout the night, while adults seem to sleep through?

The truth is, all humans rouse through the night. We sleep in cycles, with different stages of various "depths," and at the end of each complete cycle, we naturally rouse to "check" our environment. We are checking for safety, both internally and externally, though it's rare that we, as adults, consciously remember each check. Instead, it's likely that we're safe and have no pressing needs to meet, so we transition to the next sleep cycle without fully waking. Sometimes, though, we might notice a need, such as thirst (for example), at which point we would rouse more fully and meet this newly presenting need by getting ourselves a drink, before falling back to sleep again. Such wake-ups are generally noneventful and are rarely even thought of or discussed the next day. As functioning adults, we simply notice and meet these nighttime needs as they present, without concern.

For our babies, though, who are also sleeping in cycles that are fragmented into stages, nighttime need-meeting is not self-contained. They need *us* to respond to and meet their needs, as they present, and herein lies the potential for parental fatigue and concern. Because we do, often, notice and remember our babies' wake-ups the next day. Many of us track these wakes in apps, or make detailed notes to try to decipher a hidden code and find a solution to what feels like a problem in need of a fix. Moreover, we can also internalize these normal patterns of wakefulness, blaming ourselves for something that is fully explainable by biology.

"He just wakes so often!" I'm chatting to a friend on the phone.

"If he would sleep longer than a few hours, I'd feel like a new person! But he's waking after every sleep cycle. It's like he cannot join them!" Her exasperation fills the air.

So many of us have been where my friend was, wishing for longer stretches of sleep and worrying about this idea of joining, or linking, sleep cycles. Yet a baby waking after a few hours of sleep *has* joined several cycles in a row, because infant sleep cycles are, again, different from adult sleep cycles. In adults, each complete sleep cycle lasts around 90–120 minutes, while in infants, cycles are much shorter. In our youngest babies, cycles of *up to* 50 minutes are typical,[14] stretching to 60 minutes by 12 months, and 90 minutes by age five. Just as our little ones mature and develop, so too do their sleep cycles. And, when a baby rouses at the end of a sleep cycle, it's normal for an automatic "check" to take place:

Does the environment feel safe?

Is the sleep space still comfortable?

Are there any bodily sensations that need addressing, such as hunger?

Is it still nighttime?

Are physical systems regulated?

If any of these "checks," or queries, don't "pass the test," infants are innately driven to seek assistance to remedy or address whichever checkpoint is flagging. This assistance might take the form of a quick feed to fill a hungry tummy or a blanket to warm cold toes. It might also consist of closeness via a cuddle or gentle resettling via soothing words. With resettling such as this, many parents fret that the wake-up wasn't "real" or didn't amount to anything significant, but for baby, your proximity and soothing words are working their magic. Because of all the "checks" taking place, closeness is going to tick almost every single box. Closeness is a superpower, providing safety, comfort, and regulation. It meets both internal and external needs. It is, in no uncertain terms, hugely significant.

"Okay, but am I not causing him to wake by giving in and going to him every time?" My friend's question is a question that most of us have wondered, usually at 2 a.m. on a particularly wakeful night.

I pause before answering, unsure of how to say what I need to say, in a way that she needs to hear it.

"You're not causing his wakes," I begin, "You're facilitating his sleep."

Years ago, when my eldest was brand new, a seasoned mother looked me in the eye, unflinching, and told me that met needs dissipate. She said it so matter-of-factly, as if it was the most obvious thing in the world. Yet at the time, in the whirlwind of postpartum, it felt like a revelation.

Met needs dissipate.

The idea is so simple, and the words so needed. They remind me, still, to trust the child in front of me. They remind me to believe their cues and signals and needs, as and when they crop up. They remind me that needs are there to be met and that a baby, toddler, or preschooler who is waking at night is not doing so via forward planning or manipulation.

The truth is, the brain development and maturation that's *necessary* for such logical reasoning and planning is still years away. Instead, our little ones are waking because they are not yet self-sufficient with their own need-meeting, so they depend on us to keep them safe, comforted, and regulated, night and day. Doing so does not negatively impact their sleep, and it certainly doesn't lead to extra, unnecessary waking. It simply facilitates the natural pattern of sleep that occurs seamlessly when all safety "checks" are set to green.

You are not causing the wake-ups with your need-meeting. You are facilitating safe, comforted, and regulated sleep.

■ ■ ■

You are four days postpartum, and a steady stream of visitors are arriving at your doorstep to meet your newest arrival.

"Is she a good baby?" They smile as they ask, "Is she sleeping through?"

You laugh and shake your head. She's four days old, after all.

Fast-forward to four weeks postpartum, and the stream of visitors has slowed to a trickle.

"Is she a good baby?" The questions are the same, "Is she sleeping through?"

You manage a smile and shake your head. She's four weeks old, after all.

The weeks turn into months and the visits have all but stopped. From time to time, you bump into an acquaintance at the store.

"Is she a good baby?" They always want to know, "Is she sleeping through?"

You nervously shake your head and are met with raised brows. *So-and-so's baby is sleeping through*, you can hear the words but you're not really in the conversation. *It's time to nip the wake-ups in the bud*, you're told. *Sleep is important*, you know. She's four months old, after all.

■ ■ ■

"Sleeping through the night" is pitched to us as the ultimate goal. It's a target to hit, as quickly as possible. A "must" for these early years.

But what exactly is sleeping through? Can we quantify it? Justify it? Explain it? And should we be aiming for it, above all else?

Overwhelmingly, we tend to think of "sleeping through" as one continuous stretch of sleep, lasting 12 hours, from 7 p.m. until 7 a.m., which happens consistently, night after night.

This elusive 12-hour stretch is sold to us as the "best" sleep out-come amid an array of worse, or even "wrong," outcomes to avoid. We're told, sometimes implicitly and at other times, in no uncertain terms, that it is our responsibility as "good parents" to teach our babies how to reach this goal of sleeping through. And we're warned, sometimes implicitly and at other times, in no uncertain terms, that if we do not successfully teach our children this skill of lengthy sleep consolidation, they (and us) will inevitably suffer.

(No pressure, though.)

When we strip away the "shoulds" and focus on the biology of how babies sleep, it quickly becomes clear that "sleeping through" for 12 solid hours at night is a generic goal that's fundamentally flawed. Because sleep is not a skill to teach. It is, instead, a homeostatic process that happens autonomously, much like breathing and digestion. And when we consider the way in which human sleep is structured, we can see that the very architecture of baby sleep rests on and relies on rousing, to ensure safety and regulation.

When babies rouse from deeper to lighter sleep, and to partial or full waking if needed, they are experiencing a very normal and protective feature of sleep. This rousing helps ensure calorie input, maintain oxygen sufficiency, and, in turn, can help protect little ones against SIDS.[15] To push for a 12-hour, uninterrupted stretch overnight is to ignore these very real and beneficial nuances of rousing.

"I brought her into my bed because it was the only way she would sleep," I'm chatting with a mom who's feeding her baby, "But now I feel like I'm triggering her wake-ups, just by being so close!"

Honestly? This mom might be right. And the nuance here is that this *triggering* is likely a very, very good thing.

We call this kind of environmental disturbance an "externally induced arousal," and it's incredibly common among bed-sharing moms and babies. It's not truly causative of a wake, since baby's sleepy rousing was already primed to happen, driven by the human biological drive toward safety and regulation, yet the word "trigger" speaks volumes.

Specifically, moms who sleep near their babies tend to do so face-to-face. The "cuddle curl" position is often suggested for bed-sharing pairs, where mom's body *and breath* can safeguard baby. How? By the physically protective "cocooning" facilitated by the curled positioning, of course, but also via the slightly elevated level of carbon dioxide that's emitted from mom's outbreath. This elevation can trigger baby to rouse and therefore reduce the risk of arousal deficiency.[16] Remember, though, rousing doesn't automatically mean a full wake, an hour spent pacing, or a lengthy feed; it results in a "check" where baby scans for internal and external safety and regulation. This allows for need-meeting, should a need present, so we can think of this external "trigger" as a mechanism through which biology offers up a little extra protection, if it so happens to be required.

"All done?" The mom is asking her baby, who has stopped feeding and is now falling asleep in a post-milk haze.

"It's like this all night, too," she shakes her head in disbelief, "I know I shouldn't be feeding her to sleep, but what else can I do? She's never going to sleep through at this rate!"

The "shoulds" are many in the world of baby sleep, but most of them are redundant, and this one in particular is notoriously problematic because milk and sleep go hand-in-hand during the early years. A baby falling asleep during or after a feed is not a baby with a sleep problem; she's a normal human baby doing normal human baby things, and these things are not inherent blockers of the whole family getting a restful, peaceful night's sleep.

This is where a definition of "sleeping through" would help, because for every parent sharing their disbelief at feeding through the night instead of sleeping through the night, there's another who is adamant that their night-feeding baby sleeps through, *with just a few feeds*.

To gain a little clarity and perspective, then, it can help to look back at where the goal of "sleeping through" originated, and when we do this, we find ourselves landing firmly in the 1950s.

The fifties marked an era where babies were predominantly fed cow's milk–based formula and supplemented with cereals early. Babies were also more likely to sleep on their tummies, in a separate room from their parents. These points may not seem significant, but feeding and positioning can impact a baby's sleep in notable ways. Specifically, formula milk (and cereal) takes longer to digest than breast milk, which can result in fewer feeds throughout the night. Prone sleeping, meanwhile, can induce dangerously deep sleep states, which we now safeguard against with routine advocacy for setting babies down to sleep on their backs, not their tummies.[17]

In the 1950s, then, a study[18] was published that aimed to determine the frequency of night waking during infancy. In the study, parents of 160 babies were asked to log and report their babies' night waking, and of the babies taking part, 70 percent were said to have stopped night waking by three months of age. Seventy percent. The majority of these babies were said to be sleeping through by just three months; does that feel a little unlikely to you? If so, you're correct to be dubious, because what's rarely discussed, aside from the questionable accuracy of the self-reported data, is that the researchers defined sleeping through the night as a *five-hour stretch* of sleep that took place between the hours of midnight and 5 a.m.

Nowhere was a 12-hour stretch from 7 p.m. to 7 a.m. mentioned or considered. And just to really put things into perspective, there was no data reporting that these babies "slept through" regularly or continually. In fact, *almost half* of the babies who met the study's definition for sleeping through at three months had *resumed night waking* later that year (between five and nine months specifically).

Nevertheless, the seed had been sewn. "Sleeping through the night" had become a concept that quickly found its way into parenting guides and dinner conversations, and a precedent was set that persisted for decades and remains strong today. The language stayed the same, "sleeping through," while the timings stretched out. Firstly, from five hours to eight hours, occurring at any point during the night. And then, a new "family-congruent criterion" was identified, which consisted of eight hours of uninterrupted sleep from 10 p.m. until 6 a.m.[19]

Fast-forward to today and though we do not see 12 hours touted in academic literature as an achievable or desirable goal for babies to sleep, the idea of "7 'til 7" has taken root in our cultural narrative, and any family not experiencing these 12 hours of absolute, uninterrupted sleep overnight, is told, sometimes implicitly and at other times in no uncertain terms, that we have caused our babies' night waking and that we are, by default, to blame for the fact that they aren't yet "sleeping through."

The mom holding the milk-filled, blissfully sleeping baby scans her daughter's sleepy face.

"She might never sleep through," she half-laughs, "But 12 hours is a lot, right? I'm 32 years old, and I don't think I've ever slept a full 12 hours!"

The mom's shoulders relax, and she grins as she reaches into her bag to retrieve a sandwich, packed and ready to eat.

"I'm always too hungry," she laughs, taking a bite, "Like mother, like daughter, I suppose!"

■　■　■

"Oh, I think they're the same age!" A bright and bubbly mom turns to you in the line for coffee while her baby sits quietly in the stroller.

"Isn't this age incredible?" Her eyes are sparkling, "They're pointing and clapping, and they finally start sleeping so we don't have all that extra worry!"

You notice time begin to slow and a wave of heat sweeps through your body. This age has been the hardest yet. Yes, your baby points and claps from time to time, but she also wakes to feed four times a night and fights her naps with every ounce of her being. You are tired. Your eyes are not sparkling, and this coffee isn't a nice-to-have pick-me-up. It's essential fuel for soldiering through another 24 hours of incredible waking, nap-fighting, and hand-clapping.

The sweet little unicorn sleeper in the stroller begins to clap, as if on cue, and you're brought back to reality.

"Oh, yeah it's the cutest age," the words get stuck leaving your mouth, "But sleep isn't really happening for us. . . ."

Your voice trails off and you will your mouth to curl into a smile, knowing for sure that your eyes won't follow suit.

"Really?" Bright, bubbly concern meets you, and the friendly mom smiles through awkwardness.

"We need our sleep because she's prone to getting overtired if not, but all babies are different, so try not to worry," she offers.

But it's too late, because you're already there.

■　■　■

Worry and sleep tend to go hand in hand in the early years.

We are told, over and again, about the importance of sleep for growth and well-being, and we're warned about the detrimental effects of sleep deprivation on both children and parents alike. And it's true; sleep is essential for our health. It functions to support memory processing,[20] motor processing, learning, and cognitive development. It benefits the immune system,[21,22] metabolism, and growth. It even plays a role in emotional and psychological processing; it's a big deal, and true clinical sleep deprivation carries risk.

Yet, there is a difference between clinical sleep deprivation and nighttime wake-ups in infancy. Because just as sleep serves a purpose and a function for our littlest humans, so too does night waking. Rousing helps keep babies safe overnight, maintaining oxygen levels and facilitating adequate calorie input. For breastfeeding duos, night feeds support mom's milk supply and offer baby a built-in biological mechanism for falling back to sleep more easily. This is because breast milk is abundant in sleep-inducing compounds, which act to facilitate sleep in the moment and help develop and mature baby's circadian rhythm overall. Sucking, too, be it breast or bottle, is inherently relaxing for babies, serving to support sleep after normal nighttime rousing, without issue.

When we flip the script and view both sleep and rousing as functional, it becomes far easier to trust that we haven't caused the wake-ups and rest in the knowledge that they're *meaningful* features of infancy, not a recipe for disaster or overtiredness.

This idea of overtiredness is one that circulates mothers' groups and playgrounds and social media comment sections without pause, and it's at the root of a sizeable portion of parental worry. We worry not only about the potential negative impact of overtiredness, but also about whether we have caused it, by "failing" to get our babies to sleep before their telltale tired signs begin to present.

After all, shouldn't "Good Parents" do everything in their power to ensure that their babies are well rested? And isn't a well-rested baby one who naps for hours each day and sleeps 7 'til 7 overnight?

Not quite.

It is, of course, our role as parents to support our babies' development. And it is, of course, also our role as parents to respond to our little ones' tiredness and support their sleep. Whether that means pushing back morning nap because baby isn't sleepy yet or heading to bed a little earlier in response to earlier-than-expected yawns and grouchiness, we can adapt to ensure that our children's sleep is facilitated with sensitivity and flexibility.

But we are not, by any means, "failing" if our little ones become overtired after a busy day. And we are still, without a doubt, "Good Parents" if a nap is delayed, or if the night sees multiple wake-ups.

Because nonclinical overtiredness is a part of life. We all experience it; perhaps we took on an extra shift and ended the day feeling grumpy and "spent." Or through a more positive lens, perhaps we met friends for dinner and stayed up late, only to return home feeling extra tired, but overall content. Another word for this day-to-day overtiredness is dysregulation; it's when we've pushed ourselves just a little too far, past our usual window of tolerance, and we're running low on energy. Can this be unpleasant? Sure. But is it a crisis, typically? Absolutely not. We simply "refresh and renew" the next time we settle down to sleep. Because sleep is restorative by nature, so our overtiredness is remedied and regulated via the very next sleep we take.

Our babies are no different; they, too, will show grumpiness when their systems are dysregulated by tiredness that creeps over the normally tolerated threshold. We see this, often, during transitions such as nap drops, when there are fewer opportunities to restore and renew being taken throughout the day, with longer periods of waking in between sleeps. This tiredness level is referred to as sleep pressure, or the homeostatic sleep drive, and it pairs with the circadian rhythm to drive our need for sleep.

The higher the sleep pressure, or tiredness, the more sleep is needed, and the easier it is to facilitate.

The lower the sleep pressure, or tiredness, the less sleep is needed, and the harder it is to facilitate.

So, if sleep pressure gets especially high, biology offers us a compensatory mechanism to stabilize and regulate our bodies. That is, we tend to see an increase in cortisol levels. This is nature's way of keeping us alert and responsive until it is safe and appropriate for us to fall asleep. In our evolutionary past, this would have kept us physically safe when we grew tired hunting. It wouldn't have been safe or appropriate to nap on open plains, so instead, a release of cortisol would have given us a "second wind" to help us get back to camp, ideally with dinner.

Nowadays, cortisol gets a bad rap. We speak of it as the "stress hormone," and since we are told that stress is inherently bad, it's easy to assume that raised cortisol levels are concerning too. But biologically speaking, not all stress is created equal. There is such a thing as "positive stress," and with cortisol in mind, understanding its release in terms of functionality offers a refreshing perspective.

As with most things, it comes down to balance. A baby with a very high sleep pressure might push past their normative window of tolerance and become overtired. This overtiredness, or dysregulation, tends to play out as either unsettled behavior or a boost of energy (also known as a second wind and likely associated with *functionally elevated* levels of cortisol). If this boost occurs, it can become harder, not easier, to facilitate sleep, and so we tend to witness bedtime or naptime "battles" instead of an easy route into slumber. Parents often worry about long-term damage or problems from such a scenario, but the truth is, common overtiredness, or dysregulation, will be remedied with the next sleep.

With this widespread fear of overtiredness, conversely enough, families often experience the effects of *under tiredness*, or low sleep pressure. In our determination to avoid overtiredness, we're often attempting to settle our little ones when they simply aren't yet tired enough to sleep. Or, we're facilitating very lengthy daytime naps, only to be confronted with lengthy periods of wakefulness during the night. There is only so much sleep that a baby can and will take in any 24-hour period, and understanding this balance of tiredness, and how sleep pressure functions to drive sleep overall, can serve to replace worry with a much-needed sense of clarity.

Functionality is key when assessing infant sleep. Just as clapping is a function of communication and sleep is a function of staying healthy, tiredness and wake-ups are functional too. Tiredness drives and shapes sleep duration and timings, and wake-ups facilitate the "three Cs" that are so crucial for infant safety and regulation: comfort, calories, and connection. You didn't cause these innate needs; biology did. And importantly, you didn't cause your baby's night waking either. That was biology, too.

■ ■ ■

You're awake again.

You're feeding your baby in the rocking chair, while the dim glow of the night lamp paints shadows on the nursery wall. Outside, you can hear cars in the distance, and you wonder, briefly, where they're headed.

Your baby hungrily drinks her milk.

This isn't the first or last night you've spent like this. A quiet pair nestled together in a dimly lit room. There have been many nights where the quiet has been drowned out by the noise and persistence of the worries racing through your mind. The questions, the doubt, the fear. You've wondered, too many times to count, whether you're doing it right. Whether your baby should be waking this much. Whether there's any point at all to these hours spent feeding and rocking.

But not tonight. Tonight, the quiet rings out, blissfully. Tonight, you're grateful for milk and midnight gurgles and the soft sound of content little swallows as you meet a need you've decided to trust.

Once upon a time, you might have felt unsure in this moment; uncertain of where you were headed.

But not tonight. Tonight, your North Star is the baby in your arms, who pauses for a second, and glances up at you, as if to check that you're paying attention.

Your eyes fill with tears, but they are not sorry tears.

"Mama's here," you whisper, and for the first time in a long time, you feel certain that that's enough.

■ ■ ■

Pause

"My baby wakes up to feed every couple of hours through the night."

Your baby's answer: "I am growing. My stomach is still small, and I digest my milk quickly. I need regular calories, day and night, to keep up with all the growing I do. But feeding isn't just about milk, mama. It's about comfort, too. Because when I feed, my whole body relaxes. My hands, which started out curled into tiny fists, slowly unfurl. My breathing slows. My eyelids grow heavier, and before I know it, I'm drifting again, feeling warm, comforted, and soothed. One day, I'll sleep without milk, mama, and our midnight feeds will be a distant memory. One day, I won't need you quite so much at night. But for now, I do. And I love that you're here."

Prompt: How do you feel when you're awake and feeding your baby at 2 a.m.?

Rest Assured, a Nurturing Approach

Many families are advised to introduce solids early or withhold milk feeds at night with the sole aim of reducing night waking. Others are told that night feeds become unnecessary after four months or that weaning is a guaranteed way to encourage longer stretches of sleep.

But this isn't the case. Instead, night feeding remains a normal, biologically expected part of infancy.

Rather than rushing to remove night feeds, we can instead take a more responsive approach, one that aligns with a baby's individual needs while still supporting parents to get the rest they need.

Understanding the Role of Night Feeds

Feeding and sleep go hand in hand, yet there is often a mismatch between what parents are told anecdotally and what's normal in terms of our human biology. Here are some key points to bear in mind:

- It's widely accepted that baby-led night feeds are a healthy and necessary feature of the first year. Baby-led means that baby is *waking and cueing for milk*, as opposed to a parent-led feed such as a dream feed.
- Babies digest their milk quickly and depend on feeds for more than calories alone. Comfort and regulation are key components of every feed.

◆ Introducing solids early in an attempt to lengthen sleep is not backed by evidence.[23] In fact, early solids can sometimes disrupt sleep due to digestive discomfort.

◆ The act of sucking itself, via breast, bottle, or pacifier, supports physiological regulation for infants, promoting sleep.

◆ Breastfeeding at night helps maintain maternal milk supply, and nighttime breast milk contains melatonin, which supports baby's circadian rhythm.[24]

When Is Baby Ready for Solids?

Some parents are encouraged to introduce solids early to "fill baby up" for the night, but this approach is not supported by research[25] and may lead to digestive discomfort or increased night waking.

Instead, it's important to wait until baby is truly ready before introducing solid foods.[26]

Signs of readiness[27] include:

◆ Good neck and head control

◆ Baby can sit upright, without support

◆ Cessation of the tongue-thrust reflex (the reflex that pushes food out of the mouth)

◆ Baby shows an interest in food

Most babies show these signs at around six months of age. Waiting until they're developmentally ready allows for a smoother transition to solids, without unnecessary disruption to sleep.

Supporting Night Feeds (While Caring for Ourselves, As Parents)

While night feeds are normal, frequent waking can feel exhausting. Rather than eliminating feeds prematurely, we can

(*continued*)

set gentle limits or make adjustments to reduce disruption, while still ensuring baby's needs are met.

Creating a sustainable approach to night feeds:

1. **Be conscious of baby's daytime feeding pattern:** Offering plenty of opportunities for feeds during the daytime can help to "offset" very frequent night feeds. This doesn't mean forcing a schedule, but rather responding to baby's cues and being mindful not to rush daytime feeds whenever possible.

2. **Consider your sleep setup:** For breastfeeding duos, safe co-sleeping can often minimize the impact of night feeds on maternal sleep. For bottle-feeding families, keeping bottles easily accessible can help streamline nighttime wake-ups.

3. **Adjust nighttime feeding patterns if needed:** If night feeds feel excessive, gentle adjustments, such as shortening the duration of feeds or gradually stretching the time between them, can help create milk-free windows.[28]

4. **Remember that this is temporary:** Over time, babies consolidate their sleep and need fewer night feeds. Trusting the process and making sustainable adjustments, as needed, can help ensure everyone gets the rest they need.

CHAPTER 5

Your Baby Already Knows How to Sleep

"You need to teach him."

The words are said with such precision. There is a mix of certainty and nonchalance to them.

"A few nights of tears and that's it. Done. He'll sleep and you'll sleep, and you can show up as your best self again!"

You shuffle in your seat, feeling called out.

You pour your heart into your baby boy, but the tiredness feels fog-like some days. You're doing your best, but what if it's not enough?

"It's your choice!" The certainty blurs a little, "But I know what I would do."

The clarification solidifies.

You sink a little further into your seat, wishing you were back home, nap-trapped and rocking in your best chair, while your baby rests against your chest. He sleeps well there, you realize, and you wonder how to go about teaching a contact-napping, night-waking baby to settle and sleep all night in his crib. You cannot imagine leaving him to cry, but maybe there's a gentler way. Maybe you really could teach him how to sleep.

You imagine a classroom full of wakeful babies, diligently learning the theory of sleep and taking notes as needed. You laugh a little, and your friend side-eyes you briefly.

"You just might be losing your mind from the tiredness," she shakes her head, but there's a kindness to her tone. She wants what's best for you, you understand that completely, but the idea of attempting to teach an infant (who can't yet say his own name) to sleep only adds to the tired fog that you've been wading through for months.

"I'll take my chances," you offer, and you realize that it feels as though you've been walking a tightrope every day since your baby was born, where one wrong move is sure to see you fall.

■ ■ ■

There is no "one-size-fits-all" approach when it comes to raising babies or supporting their sleep. Each child is born unique, into a unique family dynamic and set of circumstances. Even the era and culture that we're born into dictates so much about how we're nurtured. Yet there is a generic rule of thumb, applicable to every baby to have ever been born, no matter the era or geographical location, and that's the fact that we cannot "teach" sleep.

Sleep, as a biological function, is simply unteachable. We do not learn it via logic, as a puzzle with various pieces or blocks to build. Much like breathing and digestion, we sleep without conscious thought or teaching. It's a function of our human biology that keeps us balanced, functional, and in a state of homeostasis. And just as our bones and muscles and brains grow and develop over time, so does our sleep architecture.

We see sleep cycles lengthen, as the early months and years progress.

We see less of a need for sustenance through the night, as tiny tummies grow.

We see fewer daytime naps taken, as babyhood turns into toddlerhood and early childhood sets in, since sleep pressure builds less acutely, over time.

These processes occur over a timeframe of years, not weeks or months. And they do so in a fluid, nonlinear way. In fact, we may experience periods of relatively little waking during the night, followed by periods of intense waking and nighttime feeds, as baby's growth accelerates during a growth spurt, for instance. Far from a lack or loss of learning, this fluctuating, evolving way of sleeping (and waking) is a biological expectation of infancy.

As such, a child who once slept in long, consolidated chunks of time, who then reverts to waking for a feed, has not forgotten how to sleep. Nor has he "unlearned" a skill that he was diligently taught. He is simply behaving in ways that elicit homeostasis. That is, he's bringing himself back to a place of biological safety, balance and harmony, perhaps via a boost of calories, or maybe through the comfort that a 2 a.m. cuddle with Mama can bring. Both are reasonable, expected, and beneficial for his development.

Yet, we are told, often, that it is our duty to give our children the gift of sleep. That we must teach them early or else suffer the consequences. We are even told that we are doing our babies a disservice by not teaching them this lifelong skill during their earliest months. But we know, from a sleep science standpoint, that this is powerful marketing at best and dangerous messaging at worst. To view sleep through a generic, "one-size-fits-all" lens is to miss the nuance of differing and fluctuating human needs.

And that's where the real gift lies. The real duty and service that we offer our babies can be found in tuning in, trusting, and meeting those needs, night and day. This isn't always easy, and some nights it's outright difficult, but it is still important.

How will our babies learn to sleep, if we're not actively teaching them, though?

This is a question that crops up often, and it's a fair question to ask, when we consider the prominent messaging around the idea of sleep training, or "sleep teaching." To answer, let's first turn back the clock by several months to a time before baby's birth.

"He seems to sleep all day," my friend rests a hand on her pregnant belly and smiles.

"Oh, wait, maybe that was a little kick," she pauses, "He must be getting comfy in his sleep."

Our babies sleep in the womb, and they do so without teaching or training. It's automatic, and though sleep patterns are not yet synchronized with the day-to-night cycle, sleep is still occurring.

"I'm not sure how to teach him that sleep is for nighttime!" My friend's hand is still resting on her rounded bump, "So far, I swear he just parties all night!"

During pregnancy and in the initial weeks postpartum, nighttime baby parties are a norm, though this doesn't mean we're collectively birthing nocturnal humans. Instead, our babies are born with unclear day–night cycles, with no strong distinction between the two at first. Newborns, for instance, spend 70 percent of their first few weeks after birth sleeping, and the timing of these periods of sleep is distributed across both day and night, without yet following a set circadian rhythm.[29] In the early months postpartum, though, the differentiation between day and night occurs, and it does so without active lessons or teaching.

Instead, the development of baby's circadian system occurs automatically, simply by living life. We term this "entrainment," which is not to be confused with "sleep training," and it requires no conscious guidance at all. Specifically, entrainment of the circadian rhythm occurs when baby is exposed to "time cues" from the external environment, and the biggest cue for our little ones is daylight.

Light regulates both mom and baby's "master clock" and in the postpartum period, the composition of breast milk also supports, and mirrors, this day-to-night divide, with melatonin levels peaking at night. This "nighttime milk" helps entrain baby's master clock, albeit indirectly via mom, while light exposure itself sends the same signals directly. For formula-fed babies, this indirect, milk-based entrainment doesn't occur, yet the direct entrainment does; the more we exist in the world during daylight hours, the better entrained our little ones' circadian rhythms will be. In this way, we are not sleep teachers, and nor are we risk-taking tightrope walkers, where one wrong move leaves us sleep deprived forever. Instead, we are "gatekeepers,"[30] tasked with enabling and facilitating the external factors that best support our little ones' master clocks and, by default, sleep overall.

■ ■ ■

"He's never going to sleep if you don't sleep train."

These words meet you at a family function, and they instantly flood your body with adrenaline.

"It's time to give him the gift of sleep," the words and adrenaline continue.

You look around the room and wonder if every person in every conversation was once left to cry it out. You question whether babies have always been sleep trained in their earliest months, or if it's a relatively new practice. Your brain plays a silent movie of a future laced with sleep deprivation and worry.

You realize, though, changing the subject as quickly as you can, that worry has already set in.

Later, you're settling your baby boy to sleep in the rocking chair. You're comfortable, though tired, and the movie loops in your brain, entirely uninvited.

"He's never going to sleep," the words loop too.

"Never."

The boldness of the statement jolts you a little, and you dare to glance down at your baby boy, who is sleeping soundly in your arms.

Is this moment, right here, somehow *wrong*? Is there something amiss with this quiet peacefulness between mother and child? Is it problematic to offer comfort and soothing at bedtime? Should you be setting him down and walking away?

"Not *never*," you breathe, and you kiss your son's forehead, to which he opens his eyes just a little, smiles, and falls back to sleep again.

■ ■ ■

Sleep training is not a rite of passage of infancy. It's an option pitched as an "answer" to sleep disruption in the early years, but it doesn't come with a guarantee, nor without risk.

Sleep training exists in many forms. Some techniques instruct parents to set their baby down in the crib and return in the morning. Others instruct parents to set their little ones down for specific intervals of time, with brief "checks" occurring in between intervals. Others, still, instruct parents to stay in the same room as baby at sleep times, but without eye contact or interaction.

On the surface, there are differences to these approaches, and the latter two are often referred to online or in mothers' groups as "gentle sleep training," yet these methods are all rooted in the belief that we can control and train our babies' sleep and behavior via disconnect and that this is desirable. From a biological viewpoint, we know that sleep is not a conscious behavior to control, and from a psychological stance, there is an array of issues that can present when we focus on behavior at the expense of feelings and needs.

Advocates of sleep training approaches are adamant that there are no long-term risks with solo crying or a lack of responsiveness at bedtime, and that such methods pave the only, best, or fastest route to achieving the elusive goal of sleeping through the night. Yet day after day and year after year, I support families who tell a very different tale. These are families who sleep trained their babies and found that it "didn't work."

There was the family who actively sleep trained for weeks at four months and were told to "cry it out" six more times before baby's first birthday.

There was the family who sleep trained at six months, expecting the process to take three days to a week, yet their training continued for six weeks before they decided to opt out.

There was the family who sleep trained at nine months and had been navigating worsening night waking and a heightened sense of separation anxiety ever since.

I have hundreds upon hundreds of stories like these, and every single one of them comes from parents who want what's best for their baby, and who have been advised that sleep training is the best and only option when it comes to infant sleep.

Yet something shocking and rarely discussed about the baby sleep industry (and it really is an industry, worth an eye-watering amount of money) is that there is no regulatory body ensuring the safety and efficacy of guidance being offered and sold to parents. This means that anybody can say they're a "Baby Sleep Consultant" and sell plans about how to sleep train, without any safeguarding against risk.

How did we get here? Let's rewind the clock again, this time to the late nineteenth century, when babies were to be seen and not heard.

In 1894, a pediatrician called Luther Emmett Holt published *The Care and Feeding of Children*[31]—a popular text that set the tone for parenting practices in the twentieth century. Inside the pages of this now-infamous book, Holt promoted the idea that babies should not be "indulged," and that if a baby cries at night when all physical needs are met, "It should simply be allowed to 'cry it out'."[32]

The age of "crying it out" was born, and the practice was more-than solidified in the 1920s, when psychologist John Watson published *Psychological Care of Infant and Child*,[33] which states of crying at bedtime, "If he howls, let him howl."[34]

Watson was a psychologist who pioneered the concept of behaviorism, a theory of learning that suggests behavior is conditioned and controlled by environmental means. He famously stated, "Children are made, not born" and believed that this "making" should be approached with the same scientific rigor as a psychological experiment. As such, his guidance for parents on parenting was both rigid and clinical:

> "Never hug and kiss them, never let them sit in your lap. If you must, kiss them once on the forehead when they say good night. Shake hands with them in the morning. Give them a pat on the head if they have made an extraordinarily good job of a difficult task."[35]
>
> – John Watson, Psychological Care
> of Infant and Child (1928)

Watson's approach was rooted in the belief that affection would undermine a child's development into a self-reliant, disciplined adult, and his views were widely shared and influential. In fact, together with Holt's teachings, they left a lasting imprint on parenting practices in the years that followed. In the 1980s, Richard Ferber published *Solve Your Child's Sleep Problems*,[36] which sold the idea that "graduated extinction" (or, leaving babies to cry at sleep times for ever-increasing time intervals) was not only acceptable and expected, but beneficial for babies.

Today, the lessons from each of these three texts linger in our cultural narrative around how we think of babies, and especially how they sleep. We are told that *good babies sleep through the night* and that independence is the goal. We are warned against spoiling infants with too much attention and affection, and to avoid *bad habits* such as rocking or feeding babies to sleep. Yet we are also at a crossroads, because although we are enmeshed within this cultural narrative, we also have a much broader and deeper understanding of the science of how and why babies behave and sleep the way they do. We know, now, that night waking is protective for babies. We know, now, that affection builds brains that are wired for relationship. We know, now, that soothing helps regulate nervous systems in support of sleep.

Perhaps most importantly of all when it comes to nap times and bedtimes and night times, though, is that we know now, categorically, that babies already know how to sleep.

■ ■ ■

You are surrounded by other mothers and babies in a waiting area.

Your baby fusses in your arms and you shush him quietly, softly rocking in your chair.

All of the other babies are asleep in their car seats and strollers, and you notice how "put together" the other mothers look.

You reposition your baby to cover a small patch of spit-up on your shirt and attempt to tame the hair that's fallen from its days-old bun.

After a lifetime, or perhaps a few minutes, the doctor calls your name and greets you with a smile. He wants to know how you're feeling and how your baby is sleeping.

You tell him that you're fine. Great, actually. So much better than fine. You smile widely and hope that your eyes don't give you away.

"Sleep could be better, though," you hear the words tumble from your mouth before you've had a chance to verify your own sharing.

"He wakes every two hours, and he feeds every single time. He settles only when he's in my arms. He's not a good sleeper."

Your filter catches up with your voice and you taper off, as the doctor nods his head and checks the time. He's heard these words before, you realize.

"You can always sleep train," he offers with a shrug, before changing the subject entirely, "Have you thought about birth control at all?"

■ ■ ■

If we compare our babies' sleep to the sleep that we'd like to have as adults, I'd guess that most of us would say we have "bad sleepers."

"Good sleepers" would settle themselves to sleep quickly and easily at bedtime, sleep through the night without a feed, and wake in the morning to freshly brewed hot coffee, right?

Yet, if we were to benchmark our idea of good or bad sleep using biologically accurate infant norms, many of our supposedly "bad sleepers" would actually chart as "good sleepers," especially when we consider the unique sleep needs of individual babies. This is because babies are born with individualized sleep needs. In fact, a variation[37] of up to eight hours in a 24-hour period can be deemed appropriate for our newest arrivals. This means that while my baby may sleep for 19 hours each day, yours may sleep for 11, and both babies' sleep totals would still likely be deemed "appropriate." Of course, there's a difference between "appropriate" and "recommended," with a variation of three hours in the first three months of life for the latter, but the fact that there is variation present at all is still incredibly important to bear in mind.

Does this mean that a baby who totals a higher number of hours asleep each day is a "better" sleeper than a baby to who falls on the lower end of the spectrum? Not in the slightest. Both are inwardly driven to meet their own sleep needs via napping and overnight stretches, and these needs will fluctuate depending on the day's activities and the child's age and stage of development. To say that there is a singular, generic, "one-size-fits-all" amount of sleep that all babies should be aiming for is simply not evidenced and can easily create more stress for families, as opposed to relief. It's futile to attempt to facilitate sleep when a baby is simply not tired enough to sleep, after all. We may end up rocking for an hour before bed or making footprints in the nursery carpet from the time spent pacing with an alert baby who's not yet ready to sleep. We might even conclude, after an evening spend actively and intentionally attempting to support sleep that never came, that our little ones must be "bad sleepers." That they must hate bedtime with every fiber of their being. That they must simply not know how to sleep.

Yet, when we zoom out and consider a baby's sleep drives, it's easy to paint a different picture. The circadian rhythm and homeostatic sleep drive work hand in hand. They exist to cue healthy sleep timings and patterns, and to build healthy and biologically reasonable degree of tiredness, or the drive to sleep. And so, the same baby who fought sleep yesterday and needed an hour of bouncing on a yoga ball in mom's arms to get close to dozing off might fall asleep without a second thought in the car on the way home from the playground today. The same baby who fidgeted through his bedtime story last night and showed no sign of sleepiness before 9 p.m. might fall asleep before closing the bedtime storybook tonight. The same baby who lay babbling quietly in his crib, long past bedtime yesterday, might fall asleep before bathtime this evening. There are moments, days, and even seasons where we are more (or less) tired, and when we adapt to the tiredness levels on display from the child in front of us, facilitating and supporting sleep becomes so much easier.

This means there is no "best" bedtime for all babies. Nor is there a singular "best" daily rhythm or routine. And just when we think we have it all figured out, a peak in development, change of season, or even a much longed for vacation can throw us for a loop all over again. And make no mistake, such loops can feel more than a little defeating when we're aiming for a 7 p.m. bedtime and a solid night's sleep, especially when we convince ourselves that this is what other, "better" sleepers are doing consistently. But the truth is, a 7 p.m. bedtime is optimal only if baby is *actually tired* by 7 p.m., and safe consolidation of sleep overnight is feasible only if baby's sleep drives are supported and optimized.

Our little ones are not "bad sleepers" if they wake when they've fulfilled their need for sleep and their sleep pressure has reduced to the extent that wakefulness is the stronger biological driver. Our babies are not bad sleepers if they resist a 7 p.m. bedtime when their bodies are still experiencing cues for alertness due to summer evening daylight pouring in from the edges of the nursery blinds. Nor are they bad sleepers when they wake to satiate a hungry tummy at 2 a.m. The biology of infant sleep explains each of these instances as healthy adaptations of being a human with human needs in an ever-growing body and ever-changing environment.

I wonder, often, how much easier these early years would be if we allowed for the nuance and grey areas. If we followed cues instead of clocks, and trusted that *good sleepers* will inevitably sleep in a range of different ways, at different times, and for different durations. Our babies already know, not cognitively, but instinctively, exactly what they need. And there's ease to be found in tuning in and trusting the nuance. Because our babies already know how to sleep.

■　■　■

You are back in the doctor's office, still wearing your unintentionally messy bun and still juggling a wide-awake baby as you field questions.

"So, how are you feeling and how's sleep going?" These same words felt weighted in the past, laden with expectation, yet today you are unfazed.

"I'm fine," carries a truth that's brand new, and you realize how long you've waited for the words to feel like they fit.

"Sleep is fine too," you reposition your baby on your lap and speak with an assured softness, "He wakes to feed and settles easily with me."

Your baby grins, as if on cue.

"He's such a good sleeper."

Pause

"My baby fights sleep."

Your baby's answer: "Some days, I'm so tired, I fall asleep in your arms before you even set me down in my crib. On other days, I don't feel quite so tired at bedtime, so you pace the floor with me in your arms, or you hold me to your chest and rock us together in our best chair. You sometimes close your eyes before I close mine, but I know you're not asleep because you check on me from time to time. I check on you too, mama. Sometimes, I smile at you, sleepily. Other times, I'm restless. I'm never restless because of you though, mama. I love when we pace and rock. I'm just not quite done with my day when the evenings stretch on. I might be working on a new skill, or I might hear older children playing in their still-light yards outside. I might even have fallen asleep in the car in the late afternoon, which feels wonderful at the time, but it eases my sleepiness enough to push bedtime back later than usual. I do love to sleep, really. Thank you for helping me drift off, mama."

Prompt: How do you feel when bedtime stretches on?

Rest Assured, a Nurturing Approach

If bedtime feels long and restless, it can help to "zoom out" and take a broader look at what's happening.

Is baby's circadian rhythm being well supported through your daily activities? Are there any extra opportunities to be outside in natural light, even for 15 or 20 minutes close to sunrise or sunset? Is baby truly ready to sleep at bedtime?

When we understand the drivers of sleep, it becomes easier to support it more effectively.

Optimizing Sleep Pressure and Circadian Support

One of the most holistic ways to support sleep is to optimize sleep pressure throughout the day.

- If baby isn't quite ready for sleep at bedtime, increasing stimulation, movement, and wakeful time during the day can help. This may mean fewer or shorter naps, or simply a later bedtime to allow tiredness to build.
- If baby is especially tired by bedtime or showing signs of dysregulation, decreasing sleep pressure by offering an earlier bedtime or more daytime sleep can help.

Ringfencing the Golden Hour

Beyond daytime rhythms, prioritizing connecting in the hour prior to sleep has been shown to improve sleep throughout the whole night.

I call this the "golden hour," and how this hour is spent is considered to be one of the most important predictors of infant sleep outcomes.

This hour includes both:

- The activities taking place, such as the features of the bedtime routine itself
- The emotional availability of the caregiver, including the warmth, connection, and responsiveness offered during this time

Specifically, a consistent bedtime routine and connection during the golden hour is associated with:

♦ Reduced sleep latency (the time it takes baby to fall asleep)
♦ Decreased night waking
♦ Increased sleep consolidation[38] (longer, more restful stretches of sleep)

To create a peaceful bedtime and support overnight sleep overall, it can help to ringfence this hour before sleep, keeping it as calm, conflict-free, and distraction-free, as possible, while building in key elements of a positive bedtime routine.

The Three Elements of a Positive Bedtime Routine

At the heart of an effective, responsive bedtime routine are three key elements:

♦ **Cues:** Predictable *signposts* that signal what's coming next. Cues help provide predictability, which can relieve stress for both baby and caregiver.
♦ **Connection:** Emotional closeness to ease the separation that nighttime can bring. Connection through rituals like a bedtime story or a favorite lullaby can help ease the transition from wakefulness to sleep.
♦ **Responsiveness:** Tuning in and responding to baby's unique needs. Responsiveness ensures that baby's emotional and physical needs are met, setting them up for a restful night.

Example Bedtime Routine

There is no one-size-fits-all, "perfect" bedtime routine, but having a gentle rhythm can help bring calm and consistency to the evening.

(continued)

Here's what a nurturing, flexible bedtime routine might look like:

- **Prepare the house:** Draw the blinds, dim the lights, and say goodnight to the birds. These activities act as a cue, or "signpost," toward the next stage of the day.
- **Offer a feed:** Breast, bottle, or a bedtime snack. Offering supper before bed helps to proactively meet energy needs throughout the night.
- **Get ready for bed:** Brush baby's teeth (if baby has teeth yet!) and consider a warm bath. While daily baths aren't usually necessary for hygiene, they can be relaxing and act as another signpost toward sleep.
- **Connect:** A 10-minute baby massage or snuggling up to read a bedtime story can be both calming and connecting.
- **Goodnight cues:** Singing a favorite song or lullaby or repeating a sleep-time mantra can help create familiarity and comfort while acting as another trusted signpost to sleep.
- **Soothing to sleep:** Supporting baby to sleep with a feed, rocking, or simply holding hands can help make the transition from wakefulness to sleep feel safe and seamless. Remember, soothed sleep is healthy sleep.

CHAPTER 6

Soothing Your Baby Is Never a Bad Habit

"Be careful."

The warning takes you off guard. Are you in danger? You scan the room but see the same old fireplace, the same old couch, and the same old side table as always.

"Be careful," the warning comes again, "You don't want to create bad habits."

A hand waves in the direction of your newborn, fast asleep in your arms, and you realize that the warning is not about an immediate threat, but a future one.

You smile the words away politely, but you feel uneasy.

Later, at bedtime, your baby is falling asleep in your arms, and you find yourself walking to her bassinet before she's fully asleep.

You lay her down.

She opens her eyes wide as soon as her back touches the sheet.

You hover, holding your breath.

She wails.

You scoop her up.

The wailing stops.

Your pulse is racing, and you can feel her heartbeat too, yet you both calm and settle together, as she sinks back into your skin, rooting for milk.

You feel better, safer even, with her close. But your mind is replaying the warning on repeat.

"Bad habits, bad habits, bad habits."

You feel guilty for prioritizing this moment ahead of the future. Are you setting your baby girl up to fail? Are you making a rod for your own back?

You don't have the energy to future-proof for bad habits tonight, you decide. Yet while your heartbeat has steadied, your breathing has slowed, and your body has relaxed, your mind still races with warnings of what might come from these moments spent soothing your baby to sleep.

■　■　■

Here is what I know to be true: there is no such thing as too much soothing. And another: comforting your baby at sleep times will not create bad habits.

How can I be so sure? Because babies thrive, biologically speaking, through soothing. They do not spoil or "go bad." (They are not fruit, after all.)

Yet we hear a different message often, don't we? We're bombarded with messaging about "too much" soothing, especially at sleep times, and it's no surprise that we can trace this way of thinking back to the turn of the twentieth century, when the "men of science" were publishing books that championed a clinical, disconnected approach to raising children.

We are now several generations deep into this way of viewing the neediness and dependency of childhood as problematic, as opposed to natural. We expect clock-following, quiet mini-adults to do as they are told and to cause no disruption to the lives of their caregivers. We fear, deeply, the idea of raising "spoiled" or "entitled" children who cannot function in the world independently. Yet we do not routinely witness teenagers climbing into the beds of their parents at 1 a.m. Nor do we commonly hear of 20-year-olds needing to be rocked to sleep.

At some point along the way, dependency morphs into independence, and the supposed "bad habits" that our babies may have grown so accustomed to in the early months and years are simply no more. They dissipate, alongside the needs that our nurture and attention were meeting.

"I know it's a negative sleep association," the mom opposite me looks down as she speaks, as if ashamed to be holding her sleeping baby in her arms.

"I do set her down sometimes," her words come quickly, "But she sleeps better this way, and we were rushing today. . . ."

Her words trail off as she fidgets in her chair.

"It doesn't look so negative to me," I offer, and for the first time in what seems like a long time, the mom breathes out.

We are told that a negative sleep association is an act of soothing or comfort that is offered to a baby at sleep times, and which is dependent on the active, nurturing input of a caregiver. For instance, breastfeeding a baby to sleep is often described as a negative sleep association. As are rocking and holding. Yet pacifiers, cribs that rock, and teddy bears with audible heartbeats are considered helpful.

From this, it becomes clear: suckling with mom is considered problematic, while suckling solo on a pacifier is sold as age appropriate.

Rocking in mom's arms is labelled as bad, while rocking solo in a "smart crib" is championed as good.

Calming to the sound of mom's heartbeat, nestled close against her body, is thought to be negative, while calming solo to the sound of a programmable teddy bear is considered positive, all round.

We are attempting to substitute human soothing with gadgets and technology, and in doing so, it becomes ever more apparent that the suckling, rocking, and calming are perhaps not the issue. Instead, the fact that our babies depend on us, as caregivers, seems to be the "bad habit" that supposedly needs remedying.

One thing is certain, though; as helpful as they may be as tools, no pacifier, crib, or bear will ever match the arms of a loving parent when it comes to soothing a baby. Because babies have evolved to be soothed via nurture-based mechanisms in a multisensory and bioactive way. That is, there is a biological feedback loop that occurs when a baby is soothed to sleep in arms. It is not simply the sound of mom's heartbeat lulling little one to sleep; it is a two-way highway of soothing and regulatory processes that happen on a cellular level between parent and child.

My breathing regulates my baby's breathing.

My temperature regulates my baby's temperature.

My heartbeat regulates my baby's heartbeat.

My voice, skin, and presence support my baby's nervous system so spontaneously that she can rest (truly and absolutely) without stress, because she feels secure.

In the simplest of terms, my calm supports my baby's calm.

And so, when we hear of "bad habits" and "negative sleep associations," it becomes important to define what a bad habit is, who it is impacting, and whether the definition is a nineteenth-century relic or a realistic, scientifically sound concept.

A bad habit, by definition, is a habit that causes problems. So, a sleep-related bad habit, by definition, is a habit related to sleep that causes problematic sleep. Soothing at sleep times will not cause problems for our babies. It will not trigger hypersomnia or hyposomnia. It will not create bedtime fears or night terrors. It will not impact a child's homeostatic sleep drive or circadian rhythm. It may not always be convenient or practical for a caregiver to offer hands-on soothing at bedtime or naptime, but from a purely sleep-science perspective, soothing will not cause sleep problems or negative sleep associations.

In fact, I would go so far as to say that connection and closeness at sleep times serve to create *positive* sleep associations for our little ones. That is, when a child feels safe and comforted while falling asleep, they grow to consistently experience sleep as a safe and comforting state to enter. Far from causing future problems, our sleep-time nurturing is paving the way for *easier* sleep in the long term.

Because if you soothe your baby to sleep, she may just get used to your comfort.

And if your baby gets used to your comfort, she may just settle well in your arms.

And if your baby settles well in your arms, she may just feel safe while falling asleep.

And if your baby feels safe while falling asleep, she may just develop a healthy relationship with sleep.

And if your baby develops a healthy relationship with sleep, she may just grow to associate sleep with feelings of calm and contentment.

And if your baby grows to associate sleep with feelings of calm and contentment, she may just sleep wonderfully, not just right now, but in the future too.

(Congratulations, that's the whole point, right there.)

■ ■ ■

There is a book by the side of your bed, which watches as you pace the room, baby in arms.

Its pages are certain that your soothing has caused your baby's night waking, and as you pace, there is a sentence that replays in your mind, on repeat:

"How she falls asleep at bedtime is how she will expect to fall back to sleep if she wakes in the night."

Your pacing quickens, but the book remains steadfast.

You worry that you have created a problem. You question whether you should enforce a stricter bedtime routine. You wonder whether you were right to have scooped your baby girl into your arms when she woke with a cry, as the clock ticked past 11 p.m.

And yet here you are at 11:15 p.m., making tracks in the well-worn carpet again. Through your wondering, you realize that your baby has fallen back to sleep, so you lay her down quietly and kiss her cheek. She stretches a little in the crib and you hold your breath, but she does not fully wake.

Slowly, you tiptoe from her crib, along your well-trodden pacing path, back to your own bed. On the way, you pass the watchful, waiting chapters on your nightstand, which simultaneously trigger your worries and promise their resolution.

But it's too late for reading tonight.

■ ■ ■

Which came first, the need or the need-meeting?

This may sound like a trick question, but there is a loud-and-insistent message, delivered to parents via books and blogs and social media pages, that the need-meeting *creates* the need.

The books tell us that bedtime rocking causes nighttime rocking. The blogs tell us that night feeds cause night-waking.

Social media tells us that being "right there" as baby falls asleep is a slippery slope toward needing to be "right there" throughout the night when baby rouses from sleep, too.

The idea that our presence and soothing could cause *more* wake-ups and less flexible settling through the night is a stark warning, but how accurate are these statements? And does biology support the warnings? What's really happening inside a baby's brain when a need is being met (or not)?

At birth, a baby's brain is still under construction, and the first three years of life are considered a *sensitive* period of brain development. Within this time, the neurons within a baby's brain are forging connections at a rapid rate, yet these connections, or synapses, are not predetermined genetically. Instead, the pathways that form are reliant on the real-life experiences of the child, and the pathways that strengthen and last for the long term are the ones that are activated and used regularly.

This is where the term "use it or lose it" applies in relation to neurological development, because the pathways that are used the least are quite literally pruned away over time. There are several episodes of neural pruning that happen throughout our lives, whereby less useful neural pathways are eliminated and more relevant ones are protected and bolstered.

We see the results of this neural pruning clearly when we compare the synaptic connections of a young child's brain with the synaptic connections of an adolescent brain, since pruning during adolescence can be both specific and pronounced. This results in a loss of up to *50 percent* of the synaptic connections in certain brain regions,[39] which raises the question: what has happened to half of a teen's synaptic highways?

Quite simply, the less utilized connections have been eliminated, while the most well-utilized connections have stabilized. This pruning process paves the way for the development of a healthy and adaptive brain; it makes sense that our brains are "wired" to adapt to the specific environment that we find ourselves in, after all, and so the "successful" pathways that remain are protected by a process called "myelination," which prevents those circuits from being pruned away.

Meanwhile, the less active synapses regress, tailoring and customizing the functional networks of the brain in alignment with the experiences that the child has lived through and within.

For babies, every time they are soothed, the circuits associated with soothing "fire up," making them more resilient to pruning, and more primed for stabilization and longevity. This is monumental work, and I cannot stress this enough: we are literally building our babies' brains with every single cuddle we give, and the positive impact of such "brain building" can be witnessed both immediately and *years* into the future. Your nurture is *safeguarding* and *future-proofing* your baby's brain.

With repeated experiences of nurturing and need-meeting, we are also wiring the infant brain for regulation. At first, we facilitate this regulatory patterning by meeting needs when they present.

We stay close to our little ones at bedtime and meet their need for connection.

We feed our babies during the night and meet their need for both sustenance and comfort.

We rock our babies back to sleep when they wake and meet their need for closeness.

Every time that we meet these needs, we are "firing up" the neural pathways that are linked to this idea of meeting a need and finding regulation via soothing. The more these pathways activate, the more built-in this pattern becomes, and over time, our babies depend less and less on our arms, milk, and presence for their soothing because their neural circuits are so well-utilized that soothing and security have become second nature.

Far from a bad habit or something to avoid, soothing shapes and primes the infant brain for health, both right now and in the future. Quite simply, the art of being able to soothe ourselves is born via instance after instance of *being soothed*.

Because if you rock your baby to sleep, she may just get used to your soothing.

And if your baby gets used to your soothing, she may just call out for you when she needs you at night.

And if your baby calls out for you when she needs you at night, she may just depend on your arms to scoop her up.

And if your baby depends on your arms to scoop her up, she may just feel soothed enough to fall back to sleep.

And if your baby feels soothed enough to fall back to sleep, she may just feel safe in her body and brain at sleep times.

And if your baby feels safe in her body and brain at sleep times, she may just grow to trust that sleep is a safe state to rest within, not just right now, but in the future too.

(Congratulations again, that's the whole point, right there.)

■ ■ ■

"Does she not self-soothe?"

The look of concern crushes you almost as instantly as the words.

"She's definitely old enough to soothe herself by now. She's six months, right?"

Your baby rubs her eyes as you rock the stroller back and forth, back and forth. She still seems brand new to you, even six months in.

Later, as you're getting ready for bed, you hear the familiar sounds of her stirring. First, the monitor screen flickers, as she fidgets in her crib. Next, her eyes open wide, searching the darkness. Then, she cries out, softly at first, but louder as the seconds tick by.

Normally, you would go and settle her straightaway. It's typical for her to wake around this time, after a couple of hours of sleep, while you wind down for the evening. This late evening resettle syncs well with your bedtime and gives you both an easy few hours of sleep before her next feed.

But tonight, you watch her fidgeting and wide eyes on the monitor, holding your breath. Her cries follow, and you question whether you should be answering them right away. What would happen if you wait it out? Might she self-soothe? Is this how they learn?

Breath-held and questioning, you creep to the nursery door, but her cries are even louder here.

"Not today, not yet" you whisper into the hallway, and in a moment your baby girl is in your arms, quiet and soothed. Albeit, not by herself.

■ ■ ■

In the 1970s, a term was coined that most of us are familiar with, even today. The term? "Self-soothing."

This terminology is said to have originated from a study[40] that was designed to non-obtrusively monitor the nighttime sleep patterns of infants, through the analysis of home-recorded videotapes. Changes in the amount of time spent in different sleep states, the duration of sleep cycles, and the time spent both in and out of the crib overall were points of interest for analysis. Importantly, the study did not set out to promote or encourage the idea of babies soothing themselves to sleep, perhaps because the concept was not pitched as a goal, but, rather, as a differentiator.

That is, within this small study into the observable sleep patterns of just 32 babies, two *types* of babies were defined: soothers and signalers.

Yet, the study did not define self-soothing in the same way that we've come to think of it. Now, when we think about self-soothing, we imagine babies who will happily and contentedly put themselves to sleep at bedtime and settle themselves back to sleep if they happen to wake during the night. We are told and sold the idea that self-soothing is a teachable skill, taught via sleep training and imperative to learn during infancy. Moreover, we are assured that in teaching our babies to self-soothe, we are in fact giving them a gift that will serve them well for the years to come.

Yet back when the research took place and the phrase was born into the world, the idea of self-soothing carried a very different meaning. In the original study, the term was simply used to differentiate between babies who signaled for parental intervention when they woke and those who didn't. Not once was self-soothing labelled as something to teach or strive for, and neither "type" of baby (signaler nor soother) was dubbed as "better" or "worse" than the other.

Imagine baby Olivia, soundly asleep in her crib. At 2 a.m., Olivia rouses from sleep and peers out into the darkness. She gets more comfortable by fidgeting and stretching a little, and perhaps even babbling to herself quietly, before drifting back to sleep again. Olivia is calm upon waking and did not signal for parental intervention to fall back to sleep. Olivia would have been labelled a "soother" in the original study.

Now imagine baby William, soundly asleep in his crib. At 2 a.m., William rouses from sleep and instantly calls out into the darkness. His calls turn to escalating cries until he is scooped up into the comfort of familiar arms, where he soon falls back to sleep again with a little rocking and some milk. William signaled his waking by crying and required parental soothing to fall back to sleep. William would have been labelled a "signaler" in the original study.

Neither Olivia nor William have sleep problems or suffer from "bad habits," and neither baby is a "bad sleeper." Even though Olivia falls back to sleep without external input, while William depends on his caregiver's soothing, neither child has been taught the "skill" of self-soothing. Perhaps most importantly of all, though, is the fact that Olivia is *already calm* upon waking. She is *not* soothing herself, or self-regulating, from a state of stress.

"She will not self-soothe!"

My friend is exasperated and tired.

"She isn't even hungry when she wakes! She doesn't want milk; she just wants me. She falls back to sleep straight away, just so long as I'm there. I don't know what I'm doing wrong."

According to the original definitions, my friend's baby girl would be dubbed a signaler, not an infant with a sleep problem. And according to the original study, there would be no "prescription" or drive to teach or train the idea of self-soothing. Yet nowadays, my friend feels like a failure. She is certain that she is missing a memo that other parents have received about how to teach self-soothing in infancy. Or, perhaps she received it and disregarded it, as the advice didn't sit well or feel aligned.

You need to be firm, the memos tell us.

Let them cry, they state.

Your baby will self-soothe only if you teach them to, the messaging tells us, without faltering.

Yet from a biological viewpoint, this is simply untrue. Because the science is clear: babies do not soothe themselves from a heightened state of stress via solo crying. The crying may stop in time, of course, but a cessation of tears does not equal soothing. Such quieting is more likely the preservation of bio-critical and essential energy in the face of acute stress.

So, if we do not teach self-soothing via firmness, solo tears, or logical teaching, how do infants develop into adults who *can* soothe themselves?

First, there are many, many adults who are yet to develop the full capacity to self-soothe and who have grown to depend on external means of soothing, such as a reliance on substances or habits that offer relief via distraction or dissociation.

For those who *have* developed robust self-soothing capabilities, that is, to self-regulate from a state of stress, we know that this healthy development occurs through thousands upon thousands of instances of *co-soothing*.

Co-[41]
Prefix: together; with

Soothing[42]
Adjective: making you feel calm

Co-soothing is co-regulation in action. It is the act of sharing our physiology with our babies, where their nervous system maps to ours, their temperature regulates with ours, and even their breathing synchronizes with ours. Our cells are primed for this sense of sharing, and our emotional states are no different. We soothe together. We find equilibrium *with* one another, until we have developed and matured enough to find such regulation solely within ourselves. And even then, the power of co-soothing does not expire. Even as adults, we can and do still benefit hugely from this sense of shared regulation, be it with a partner, or even as parents breathing in the peace and warmth of a contact nap on a rainy afternoon.

We share our calm with our babies, and in a beautiful natural feedback loop, we are also primed to benefit from that shared calm, too.

And this all happens through connection. This developmental ability to first rest in the calm of another, and then, in time, create that sense of calm within and for ourselves.

Why? Because the neural highways that are utilized most stabilize best. The more a child is soothed, the more that child develops the neural pathways primed for soothing. We can think of this as akin to muscle memory, but for the brain. At first, such soothing is entirely dependent on the caregiver, but over time, as the neural highways stabilize and are activated on repeat, such soothing becomes second nature.

A soothed child learns soothing. It is as wonderfully simple as that.

Because if you go to your baby when she cries at night, she may just need you to soothe her.

And if your baby needs you to soothe her, she may just stop crying when you pick her up.

And if your baby stops crying when you pick her up, she may just settle into your warmth.

And if your baby settles into your warmth, she may just let out a big, deep sigh.

And if your baby lets out a big, deep sigh, she may just feel safe enough to relax back into sleep.

And if your baby feels safe enough to relax back into sleep, she may just grow to associate sleep with feelings of safety, regulation, and soothing.

(Congratulations once again, that's the whole point, right there.)

■　■　■

You are sitting in your favorite chair, rocking with your baby in your arms.

She is fast asleep and the rise and fall of her little body against your chest feels like the greatest gift.

"Who's it really for, her or you?"

Words from an earlier conversation disrupt your cozy bliss. They had been said with a smirk, about your contact napping ways, and they had stung.

They still sting, now.

Yet the harshness seems to be evaporating with every glide forward and back, forward and back.

Your baby let's out a sigh. The big sigh. The sigh of safety. She is fast asleep now, you know. Yet you do not set her down in her crib, even though you could. Even though there is a mountain of chores and emails to work through, you remain there together, gliding.

Who's it really for?

It's for both of you, you decide.

In these moments, your calm calms your baby, and her big deep sigh of safety sends a wave of safety through every cell in your body, too. Your baby's soothing is your soothing and vice versa; there is no distinction needed.

Who's it really for?

It's for both of you, both right now and years from now, you're sure. These hours spent gliding together are not for nothing, you're certain. Because soothing your baby is never, ever, a bad habit.

■ ■ ■

Pause

"My baby doesn't self-soothe."

Your baby's answer: "I sleep best when I'm in your arms, mama. Or when I'm in my crib with your warm hand resting on my belly. Or even when I'm in my crib and I can hear my favorite words in the world: 'mama's here'. Every time you soothe me, I grow more and more used to feeling calm and settled and just right, but I won't always need you here, I promise. One day, I will be able to tuck myself in, settle down, and sleep without your arms, warmth or voice. But not yet, mama. I'm not ready for that day just yet."

Prompt: How do you feel when it's your closeness that soothes your baby best?

Rest Assured, a Nurturing Approach

When we think about the idea of self-soothing, it can help to first understand whether our little ones would be classified as "signalers" or "soothers."

- ◆ **Signalers:** Babies who naturally call for their caregiver when they wake, needing comfort or reassurance before settling again
- ◆ **Soothers:** Babies who, when they wake, tend to fidget, stir, or babble to themselves before drifting back to sleep on their own, without needing an active response

(continued)

If your baby is naturally a "signaler," your responsiveness to those cues and signals will help stabilize the "soothing networks" of synapses inside their brain, helping to form the foundation of their ability to self-regulate over time.

Meanwhile, if your baby is naturally a "soother" and does not signal upon waking, we can often "practice the pause" when baby wakes.

Practicing the Pause

Practicing the pause simply means watching and waiting for a few moments before going to baby when they wake.

Some babies will naturally stir, fidget, or even babble after waking in the night, without needing to be soothed by a caregiver. If there is no pressing need, many natural "soothers" will fall back to sleep on their own if they are tired enough.

The key here is observation without expectation. Rather than withholding needed comfort, practicing the pause allows us to gently assess whether baby is signaling for support or settling on their own.

The Role of Co-Soothing

Regardless of whether a baby is a signaler or soother, co-soothing is foundational for the development of self-soothing. Babies learn to regulate through us, after all.

Here are four key "sense steps for co-soothing" that can help explain how co-regulation supports self-regulation over time:

- ◆ **Physical connection:** Proximity sends safety signals that allow an infant's physiological systems to function optimally.
- ◆ **Sensory inputs:** A caregiver's familiar scent, voice, and even breathing patterns provide sensory input that supports baby's regulation.

◆ **Attunement and responsive caregiving:** Tuning into baby's unique needs and responding appropriately sends consistent signals of security, reinforcing trust.

◆ **Emotional regulation:** Looking after our own emotional well-being as parents has a domino effect on our children's ability to regulate. Pausing to breathe and creating space when needed can help us co-regulate with our little ones.

Over time, the comfort and security you provide now will become the foundation for your baby's ability to self-soothe when they are truly ready. For now, they are regulating in connection, with you.

CHAPTER 7

Clingy Babies Are Normal Babies

"He's so clingy!"

The room is filled with new faces and sweeping statements, and your baby turns away from the crowd, pressing his face into your neck.

Your hair, accidentally half up and half down, covers him like a curtain, shielding him from anything and everything that exists outside of your pairing.

"Such a mama's boy."

This isn't the first time you've heard these words, and you resign yourself to the realization that it won't be the last, either.

"Mine weren't clingy like this."

A third shot fired.

You change the subject as quickly as you can and all the while, your baby stays seemingly glued to your neck.

From beneath his hair curtain, he falls asleep, and after what feels like an eternity of small talk and judgments pass, it's finally time to unpeel your boy from your body and settle him into his car seat before driving home.

He wakes, of course, without your neck and draping hair to keep him sleeping, and you drive away from the crowd of new faces and free-flowing judgments, considering the impact of this short nap on the rest of your day. Yet as you drive, one word follows you through each junction and every turning: *clingy*.

■ ■ ■

Clingy[43]
  Adjective: sticking, staying close

The concept of clinginess during early childhood is typically pitched as a negative trait to avoid. In fact, never have I ever heard the words, "He's so clingy" being uttered or interpreted as praise. Instead, they are often combined with raised eyebrows and a shake of the heard. Yet the nuance that's so often missing from such statements is the very real fact that human infants are biologically wired to stay close to their caregivers. Babies are, by default, supposed to *cling*.

Cling[44]
  Verb: to hold, to stay close

Parents carry and infants cling; it's nature's way. We are carry mammals, after all. Yet our reliance on exterogestation to further the maturity and capabilities of our newborns means that human babies do not yet have the brain development nor the physical strength or agility to *literally* cling to their parents' bodies, like orangutan or chimpanzee infants do. Instead, human babies rely on their caregivers to facilitate such carrying and closeness, and such facilitation depends almost entirely on the attachment between caregiver and child.

This word *attachment* gets thrown around almost as often as the term *clingy* and there are different interpretations of it, depending on which circles we engage with and which corner of the Internet we go to for our blogs and parenting memes. Some will say that attachment is a style or type of parenting, dubbed *attachment parenting* and often affiliated exclusively with breastfeeding, babywearing and bed-sharing. Others will say that attachment is essentially a scorecard for life, with a set of practices to "tick off" in order to work toward a "winning" score by the time adulthood rolls by. At its core, though, attachment is neither a parenting type nor a scorecard. We can, of course, support it through acts of closeness and responsiveness, which can sometimes feel more manageable via practices such as babywearing or co-sleeping. And we can also measure attachment, clinically, with a secure attachment deemed the healthiest outcome.

Yet no singular parenting style or list of checkpoints to tick off can get to the heart of what this concept of attachment really is.

Instead, we can think of attachment as a bio-behavioral system, which exists solely to support infant safety and survival. Attachment existed long before it was defined in a textbook. It existed long before the act of parenting was classified into separate "types" with specific names, and long before clinical measurements were available. Attachment has ensured our survival and thriving as a species since the very beginning.

Our babies are clinging to stay safe.

Not to exhaust us or to be difficult.

Quite simply, to stay safe.

"He death-stares every stranger," my friend speaks over her son's head as he happily plays with stacking cups on the floor between us.

"Literally death-stares them! And then clings to me like glue if they get close!"

My friend laughs, and her baby boy smiles as he hands me a cup. We sort and stack together, calmly and without death-staring.

"You wouldn't have thought it, looking at him now, would you? Butter wouldn't melt. . ."

"Cup!"

Our attention shifts and our hearts collectively grow just a little at the pure joy that this death-staring, butter-melting, almost-toddler is experiencing from stacking two perfectly fitting cups, one on top of the other.

There is a tangible sense of "just rightness" at seeing how well the cups fit together.

At its heart, attachment involves two core behavioral systems: proximity seeking and separation protest. These two systems work and fit together, much like stacking cups, to explain why a baby might cling to a parent, death-stare a stranger, or switch from calmness to distress when faced with separation.

Proximity seeking activates during times of anxiety or when a threat is perceived. It is a baby's instinctual drive toward closeness, with the sole aim of remaining safe. Such closeness not only helps ensure physical safety but also emotional support and reassurance; this is the power of connection. The separation protest system, meanwhile, can be witnessed when a baby cries when separated from a parent, which acts as a biological signal to the caregiver to *restore closeness*. Again, this is the power of connection; our babies are driven to connect, to be close, and to cling, above all else, with their innate, deep-rooted leaning toward safety.

"I just say he likes to stay close to me, you know?"

My friend passes her baby another cup, and I nod. I know it well.

"I figure if I just smile and hold him while he clings, it might offset the staring. . . ."

Another cup is passed and stacked, another perfect fit.

"And the longer I hold him, the more likely he is to take an easy nap, so it's not all bad, you know?"

I nod again; I know this well, too.

It can feel socially awkward to smile away our babies' death-stares, but the closeness that we offer during times of unease, change, or stress, in response to our little ones' proximity seeking behaviors, acts as a buffer for our little ones. Safety, both physical and emotional, serves to facilitate growth, development, *and sleep*, and this is the equilibrium that our babies are wired to seek and rest within.

When there is physiological regulation through closeness, there is less resistance at sleep times.

When there is no need to work hard to secure closeness, sleep arrives without stress.

When there is a felt sense of safety playing out at nap times, bedtimes, and nighttimes, the transition to sleep, and the act of sleeping itself, becomes easy.

Because infants are driven to find safety through attachment; it is their biological imperative to ensure and restore closeness, above all else.

Perhaps then, it could be helpful to reframe our phrasing a little, and the way that we think of this idea of clinginess. Imagine if we switched out the word *clingy* for the word *close* or even, *connected*:

> He's so close!
>
> Look how connected he is with you!

It's hard to utter or interpret these words as anything but a compliment, isn't it? In fact, it's hard to think of this closeness and connection between a parent and baby as anything other than the positive, health-giving, perfect fit that it is.

■ ■ ■

You are closing the nursery door at bedtime when you hear a cry.

It isn't a whimper or a muttering; it's an urgent, piercing cry that stops you in your tracks.

On autopilot, you open the door and walk back to your baby's crib. You rest a hand on his belly and his cries quieten.

"Mama's here," you soothe, and he takes big deep breaths, as if recovering from the longest 10 seconds of separation ever to have taken place.

With your words and the warmth of your hand, sleep begins to overtake your little one again, and after a while, you lift your hand slowly.

Right on cue, and as if by magic, your baby's eyes open wide, in alarm.

"Mama's here," you soothe again, and your little one pauses before he lets his lids bridge together once more.

This is going to take a while, you realize, resigning yourself to the nursery floor and retrieving your phone from your pocket.

The room now aglow, you begin typing into the search bar, but the autofill function finishes your sentence before you're even halfway through the second word: "separation anxiety in babies at night."

■ ■ ■

For many babies, sleep is the most prolonged period of separation that they experience each day, and while this may not seem like a big deal to our mature brains, infants don't yet have the logical functioning capabilities that we have as adults. Logically, as adults, we know that if somebody walks out of a room, they still exist on the other side of the door, and we tend to have a good gauge as to when that person will return. This simple knowing is termed *object permanence*, and it's a milestone of the sensorimotor stage[45] of infancy, spanning from birth to two years. This means that at some point during these first two years of life, our babies develop to be able to take it for granted that we still exist even after we've left a room.

In real terms, object permanence tends to develop in the second half of the first year, which aligns to the time that separation anxiety typically peaks in infancy, too. This is no coincidence, because while our little ones are learning that we still exist on the other side of the door, they do not yet have the rationale to understand that the shutting of the nursery door does not equal the forever separation of parent and child. With an unknown duration and degree of separation at play, an alarm bell rings for our babies, and their innate, biological mechanisms to maintain and restore closeness kick into play.

This might look like clinginess or fussing as a caregiver moves away, or it could take the form of tears and calls immediately after a door closes and separation becomes a reality. We have come to refer to these behaviors as separation anxiety, but for infants, I'd go so far as to say that this terminology could use a refresh, or at least a little clarification. Because our babies are not anxiously weighing up the risks, causes, or effects of separation; they don't yet have the neural development for such reasoning. Instead, they are responding, innately and in alignment with their level of neurological maturity, to separation in a very biologically appropriate way. This reaction isn't an overreaction, even though it might look this way to our mature, logical adult brains. This reaction is, in fact, a *reasonable* reaction, all things considered.

Once upon a time, long ago, before nurseries existed and before shelters even had doors to close, the separation of a baby from their caregiver during the night would have spelled disaster. In times gone by, it wasn't a sense of comfort or preference at stake; separation represented a true threat to survival. And though our homes and societies have evolved and changed over many, many years, our babies' brains have not. For our youngest humans, separation from a caregiver still feels like disaster. It feels like a threat, and so, without conscious thought or reasoning, attachment-seeking behaviors activate as a means of survival and to downgrade the level of threat being experienced.

Dear Louise,

I think my baby has separation anxiety! He cries the second I leave his room at bedtime. What am I doing wrong?

The emails I receive act as a looking glass into the nuances and worries of parents, far and wide.

Dear Louise,

My baby suffers with extreme separation anxiety. I haven't been able to go on a date with my partner since he was born because he freaks out when I'm not there. What am I doing wrong?

Message after message, each from a unique family with a unique set of circumstances, but so often with very similar concerns.

Dear Louise,

Can you help us? My son cries for me at night. He sleeps fine when I bring him into my bed, but he gets separation anxiety in his own crib. What am I doing wrong?

My inbox bears witness to countless mentions of separation anxiety each and every week, and it's clear that each message has been sent with a mix of worry and hope. Worry about failing, about missing inherent problems, and about doing this thing called parenting *wrong.* And hope; about a fix, about finding a solution, about getting things *back on track.*

It's hard. I know, truly, I know. It's hard to be this needed. And at the same time, in most instances, babies showing signs of anxiety or protest upon separation are ever-so-healthy, developmentally tracking, *normal babies.*

Because normal babies seek proximity and protest separation.

Normal babies are innately driven toward closeness and experience an intuitive sense at alarm when separated from their primary attachment figure.

Normal babies cling, and some (still-normal) babies cling tighter, and for longer, than others.

This isn't a problem to fix; it's a biological phenomenon to understand and to work with. We do not need to stamp it out or override it with adult logic and reasoning, nor do we need to gather or attribute blame. Because blame is wholly unnecessary and irrelevant when babies are tracking along their development curve in just the way they were designed to track.

For the baby who starts crying the second the bedroom door closes, for the baby who falls asleep with mom and only mom at bedtime, for the baby who bed-shares beautifully but resists his crib with all his might, we can work with this supposed clinginess, this separation anxiety and drive for attachment. We can understand the need on a biological level first, to better equip ourselves with reasonable expectations and strategies that can support more ease and flexibility, without setting off those internal baby alarm bells at the slightest hint of separation.

Because we can act as both a safe haven and a secure base for our little ones. That's the ask when it comes to attachment. We have dual functionality as attachment figures, to offer responsive care that allows our babies to express distress at separation and to rest in the closeness of connection. In doing so, we can support our little ones' sense of exploration as they develop to exist in the world with gradually more and more separation from us, minus any sense of alarm.

It's through attachment that our babies can lean into trust, knowing at all times that they can return to us, back to the sanctuary that we spend the early years carving out, piece by piece and in the depths of the night, even when we're wracked with worry that we're somehow doing it wrong.

(We're not.)

Nurture on.

■ ■ ■

"He's too attached."

"Too attached?"

"Far too attached. He really should be fine without you by now."

You glance at the baby in your arms. The one you met nine months ago but have known a lifetime. The one your body carried and delivered and continues to nurture even now, as he thrives on the outside of your skin.

Too attached.

It sounds absurd, but it stings.

He cannot walk by himself yet, so you carry him.

He cannot fix himself a sandwich yet, so you feed him.

He cannot settle himself to sleep yet, so you soothe him.

Your mind races with what to say, with how to react, with what to offer this accusation of *too much* attachment, but nothing feels quite right.

So instead, you shrug and shake your head to brush away this warning of *too much*, but the words linger, unshaken.

Later, as you're feeding your baby to sleep, you wonder what becomes of babies who are *too attached*. You wonder whether well-attached baby boys really do turn into mama's boys, and then you stop yourself from wondering any further.

There are worse things, you decide.

"So be it," you whisper, mostly to yourself, and your baby sighs deep, as every perfectly created cell of his body rests peacefully in your arms.

■ ■ ■

There is no such thing as too much attachment.

That is, babies cannot be too attached.

Because attachment is not measured in pounds or ounces. It does not ever overflow or spoil from excess. Instead, attachment is typified at the highest level as either secure or insecure.

With a secure attachment, our babies can rest and grow safely within it. They can depend on it, expect it, rely on it. With an insecure attachment, though, a child's in-built bio-behavioral system, which is primed for safety and survival, is threatened.

An insecure attachment undermines a baby's thriving, yet babies cannot opt out of forming attachments. Attachment exists to support the safety and survival of our species, after all, and so when there is misattunement or misalignment between parent and child, the child does not walk away from or "quit" the relationship. They cannot; our babies are entirely dependent on us to survive and thrive. Instead, little ones do the best they can with the attunement and alignment that's available to them, and when the sensitivity and responsiveness of an attachment figure is consistently erratic, dismissive, or a-typical during times of distress, attachment still exists, albeit insecurely.

The strange thing about attachment classifications, patterns, and behaviors is that they are widely misinterpreted and misunderstood. A baby who clings to mom in a crowd of people is demonstrating one variation of a perfectly healthy and expected attachment behavior, staying close to his safe person in an environment filled with unknowns. A baby who cries out in alarm when he wakes alone in his crib is quite simply a baby acting to reinstate the closeness that keeps him thriving. A baby who is new to daycare and doesn't settle well without mommy at nap time is a baby who has forged a positive and secure association between the comfort that his primary attachment figure offers and sleep.

None of these examples are a cause for concern. These are all babies demonstrating behavior patterns of a healthy, secure attachment. These little ones have grown to rest in the comfort and closeness of their primary attachment figures and will display separation protesting and attachment seeking behavior patterns when such closeness is threatened or unavailable. Yet, to some commentators, these behaviors are problematic. Parents are warned, often, that clingy babies are manipulating us with their insistence on closeness. We're cautioned that dependent babies are the worst sleepers. We're told that babies who are held close are held back. Our normal human babies' attachment-seeking behaviors are all too often incorrectly labelled as signs of too much coddling, too much attention, or too much attachment.

Too much, too much, too much.

Again, there is no such thing as too much attachment.

We have decades of research[46] pointing to both the immediate *and* long-term outcomes of a secure attachment, even with innate behavior patterns that might be uncomfortable to witness or which might dislodge the social status quo.

The data shows that a secure attachment leads to higher self-esteem, better emotional regulation, enhanced social competence, greater academic success, and more satisfying future relationships. In the realest terms, a secure attachment, established through consistent and responsive caregiving in infancy, is foundational for future health and well-being. It safeguards children, acting as a buffer to life's inevitable stressors and upheavals. In just the same way that closeness brings instant relief and security during babyhood, the sense of foundational safety that secure attachment builds, brings relief and security during adulthood, too. Mama's arms may be gone, but the dependable, expected, and reliable sense of safety lingers.

"How do I do it, though?" My friend messages me as she rocks, baby in arms, back and to, back and to, from their well-worn rocking chair.

"How do I build a secure attachment?" My phone pings again with the golden question.

"You're doing it," I type back, "You're doing it right now."

It may not seem like much, or perhaps sometimes it feels like a lot; to hold and rock and hold some more as the evening slips by and our little ones drift off to sleep. But make no mistake, *this is important work.*

Because attachment is built through sensitive, responsive caregiving.

That means showing up, over and again, with care that meets needs and that offers a sanctuary to rest within.

It means trusting all needs, even the ones we cannot see.

It means allowing our children to *rest* in our arms.

We are tasked with raising independent adults who are capable, who exist within healthy relationships, and who feel innately safe within themselves. And to do this, to go about this rather huge task, we must first build that inner world, the inner trust and the inner knowing, piece by piece, from the ground up.

Every time we respond to a cry.

Every time we hold them close.

Every time we soothe them to sleep.

We are building a secure attachment and safeguarding their future.

"That's all well and good. . . ." Another message.

"But how do I avoid creating a sleep problem with all of this rocking?!"

This is the question that lingers, but when we understand the significance of attachment, of building it from the ground up in these early years, it quickly becomes apparent that any notion of a *sleep problem* from *too much* rocking or holding or supporting sleep is simply that: a notion, an idea, a culturally created warning that is not based in biological truth.

Because securely attached humans, of any age, are set up to sleep *well*. Securely attached humans are best equipped to enter sleep in safe and appropriate ways, and rest and restore until waking. Why? Because a secure attachment equates to biological safety, and when our bodily systems are not faced with threat or alarm, they do what they do best: function well, efficiently, and with ease.

Sleep is an excellent example of this. When we support those feelings of safety, by allowing our babies to settle and rest within attachment, their little bodies can truly surrender to their tiredness and fall asleep, stress free. At first, this tends to require external input, be it rocking or holding or simply having a trusted attachment figure *right there*, but in time (and really, it's just a blink of time when we zoom out), our dependent little sleepers develop into independent bigger sleepers. And nowhere along the way have we created a sleep problem. Instead, our babies have experienced sleep in positive terms, as a state that reminds them, on a deep, cellular level, how it feels to be rocked, held, and to have their person be *right there.*

"I could set him down but I'm going to linger. . . ." Another ping.

"He's clingy, but he's also comfy. . .and so am I."

■ ■ ■

You are sitting in the dark while your friends enjoy a meal out together.

"I can't make it," you'd told them, "I have plans."

A semi-lie, perhaps, because these were your plans. To sit in the dim glow of the nightlight, baby in arms, waiting for him to fall asleep, before spending the evening watching both the television screen and the monitor screen interchangeably.

You imagine other moms, offering a breezy, "Just set him down and call if you need me," as they leave the house to spend the evening with friends. But you've not uttered those words yet, in all these months of missed meals and declined invitations, because for your baby, only your arms will do.

He squirms a little, getting comfortable, and you readjust your hold and breathe out.

"Only Mama will do," you whisper the words into the darkened room, and they feel like a gift and a cage, simultaneously.

He opens his eyelids a little, catches your gaze, and smiles the most perfect smile.

Being his chosen person feels a little easier with a smile, you decide. And so, you get comfy, too, repositioning his sleepily draped legs a little as they rest against you.

Weren't they smaller yesterday? Has he grown overnight? Soon, he won't fit against you in the way that he fits so seamlessly now. The realization hits you and takes you off guard. This isn't forever, you know. And that truth brings both relief and heartbreak, all at once.

"Only Mama will do," you breathe the words again, and you trace another smile from within the darkness.

The future is built here in this moment, you know, but it can wait a while longer, because for now, you have plans.

■ ■ ■

Pause

"My baby won't accept anyone else at bedtime."

Your baby's answer: "I know it's hard, after a long day, to sit rocking with me, mama. I know you'd love to tag daddy in and take a little time to exist in your own skin, without needing to hold and soothe and rock me. I love when daddy sings to me at bedtime, too, I really do. But tonight, mama, I need you close. I promise I won't need you like this every night, and I promise it won't be long before you can set me down with just a kiss and a 'goodnight'. In the future, the evenings will be yours again, not ours. We won't spend so long sitting in this quiet, dark room together, and I'll need your arms, rocking, and soothing less and less. But right now, here in your arms, everything in the world feels right and I can drift off to sleep without a worry. Soon, I won't need your arms, your voice, or your presence quite so intensely. But tonight, mama, I need you close."

Prompt: How do you feel when your baby settles best with you?

Rest Assured, a Nurturing Approach

When children can *rest* in a secure attachment, rather than having to fight for, carve, or seek it out, sleep is supported at a foundational level.

Without a constant and insistent drive toward safeguarding, the parasympathetic nervous system activates, and human biology switches away from "fight or flight" to "rest and digest." This biological state of safety is what allows sleep to unfold with greater ease.

(continued)

Attachment, built through sensitive and responsive caregiving, is foundational to restful sleep. We can nurture this security by:

- **Giving a "yes" before it's asked for:** Offering an extra bedtime story or cuddle before it's requested can proactively reinforce a sense of safety.
- **Meeting needs without delay:** Responding promptly helps little ones feel secure and prevents heightened distress.
- **Lingering a little longer:** A few extra moments of closeness at sleep times can ease the transition into sleep and support a felt sense of safety.

Navigating Parental Preference At Sleep Times

It's common for babies to gravitate toward their primary attachment figure at sleep times, since this person is their "default" safe haven.

This is nobody's "fault" and at its core, this parental preference is actually a marker of a robust and secure primary attachment; this is a good thing.

Often, though, flexibility around who soothes baby at nap times, bedtime, and throughout the night is wanted or needed. The key to helping little ones accept a different caregiver at sleep times is to support their sense of *security* as they approach sleep.

Two concepts that can help ease this transition are bridging and checkpoints.

Bridging the Gap

Bridging creates a connection, or bridge, between "right now" (when you're physically present with your child) and "later" (when you will be together again after a period of separation).

We can build this bridge with physical items or symbolic, playful ideas, depending on your little one's age and stage of development, such as:

- A photo of you to kiss goodnight
- One of your T-shirts used as a lovey
- A picture of a drawn heart to hold onto
- Placing a kiss into the palm of your hand and "sprinkling" it over your child

Even when you're not physically present, the connection remains, tangible and reassuring in a way that's easy to grasp.

Creating Familiarity and Predictability With Checkpoints

Checkpoints are the familiar "signposts" of a routine or rhythm, which offer a sense of familiarity and security to children as sleep approaches.

For another caregiver to support sleep, it can help to:

- **Facilitate the same checkpoints that baby is already familiar with:** Following the usual checkpoints in the usual order taps into the familiarity of existing sleep associations. Bedtime checkpoints might include a bath, pajamas, story, and song, for instance.
- **Mimic familiar soothing techniques:** If there's a specific soothing style that baby is familiar with already, it can be helpful to replicate this. For instance, if baby is accustomed to motion or high sensory input at sleep times, sleep is likely to arrive more easily when these elements are present, even if another caregiver is providing them.

(continued)

It's important to note here that different caregivers will inevitably have different ways and styles of soothing babies. As an example, many families find that a breastfed baby who only ever nurses to sleep with mom is very accepting of being rocked or sung to sleep with dad. The key is that soothing is offered, even if it differs slightly to baby's normal bedtime experience.

The goal isn't to force a rigid bedtime handoff but to trust baby's cues and respond in a way that feels both responsive and flexible, even (and especially) if your little one could easily be described as *clingy*.

CHAPTER 8

Your Baby Isn't Like the Others

"She's so sensitive!"

Your mother-in-law shakes her head in exasperation.

"With each of mine, we just set them down and that was that; they slept!"

You laugh at the thought of such ease.

"This little lady needs the stars to align, don't you, Miss?" Grandma smiles with a mix of disbelief and amusement, and your baby grins back, blissfully unaware of just how rare and fleeting instances of star alignment can be.

Later, in the depths of the night, you find yourself glancing out of the gap in the blinds of the nursery window. The night sky is awash with stars, casting their light across you and your girl, who is feeding in your arms.

You wonder whether sleep really was so easy for your mother-in-law when she was a new mom or whether hindsight has been working its magic in her recollection. You wonder whether Grandma's babies ever needed soothing at bedtime, be it a cuddle, a feed, or a solid 30-minute stretch of pacing. Did *all* her children really fall asleep in their cribs without so much as a lullaby?

Your baby unlatches and squirms a little. That's your cue to begin pacing, so you rise from your comfy spot and begin part three of your nightly ritual of holding–feeding–pacing to soothe your sensitive girl back to sleep.

Yet as you pace, you can't help but feel as though the stars are winking at you through the gap in the blinds.

■ ■ ■

"She notices everything."

I'm sitting across from a mom who is bouncing her baby on her lap.

"She should be napping right now, but she has some major baby FOMO happening."

FOMO, or Fear Of Missing Out, is more common than we might assume during infancy. Our babies are wired and driven to engage with, and learn from, the world around them, after all.

"She's fussy, that's what it is," the bouncing continues, "And *so sensitive.*"

Truth be told, I knew this baby was sensitive before the declaration came. Her wide and watchful eyes hadn't faltered with their acute and unwavering observation of me and the new space from the moment she'd been carried into the room.

"And when she doesn't like something," the mom shakes her head slowly, "Oh my goodness, do I know about it!"

Highly sensitive babies, just like highly sensitive children and highly sensitive adults, are humans who feel and process the world more deeply than average. They tend to have intense reactions to the stimuli of the environment around them and will often let us know, loud and clear, when something (internal or external) is amiss. They are life's observers, with near-hyper awareness at times, and as such, they tend to become easily overstimulated in busy environments. Often born wide-eyed and watchful, they're the ones waking with the slightest change in temperature overnight, and the ones easily alarmed by a dog's barking two blocks away. They seem to feel everything, in all the ways, all the time; and they feel it intensely.

This has its challenges, of course, but it also offers an array of benefits. Our world needs highly sensitive humans just as much as it needs less sensitive humans. We need individuals who notice the nuance, who feel and process deeply, who can pause and assess before leaping in. With this in mind, sensitivity can be thought of as a survival strategy for our species; with 20–30 percent[47] of the population genetically predisposed to sensitivity, or *responsivity* as it is sometimes termed. It's even accepted that those who are less sensitively wired rely on their more sensitive counterparts to notice, process, and learn from life's subtleties, and in this way, sensitivity is said to help safeguard entire communities.[48,49]

For individuals, too, there are great benefits that sensitivity can bring. Empathy, understanding, and the existence of a rich and creative inner world are commonly associated with high sensitivity.[50] Yet, with such deep processing of sensory stimuli and input, and with such acute awareness of the world around them, highly sensitive babies are often more wakeful and harder to soothe than less sensitive babies. It really can feel as though the stars need to align for sleep to occur.

The room's temperature needs to be just right.

The onesie needs to be fitting just so.

And Mama needs to be just there.

Any deviation from the usual and accepted bedtime rhythm, or any variation in sleep setup, sickness, travel, or a different way of soothing, can disrupt sleep to such a degree that parents are often left feeling as though there must be a rare, deep-set sleep problem to solve, especially when fielding tales of other babies who happily settle and sleep without fuss, no matter what.

"Your baby isn't like the others," I offer these words often, and then I pause and assess how they land.

Because this idea of *difference* can feel alarming, if not properly understood. We are told, time and again, that *all babies* should be soothed a certain way and sleep for a certain number of hours each night. To attempt to fit *any baby* into this predetermined supposed ideal is tricky, at best, yet with a highly sensitive baby, it can be entirely futile. Because our highly sensitive little ones have nervous systems that operate with a different level of responsivity. Their brains process information more deeply, reflecting on and reacting to stimuli that others might overlook. With sensitive little ones, generic sleep plans and nontailored soothing methods are more likely to result in longer bedtimes and more frequent night waking. Why? Because sensitive babies will notice even the tiniest degree of misattunement between their internal state and their external environment; if they are experiencing the slightest pang of hunger or the mildest sensation of discomfort and are placed in their cribs with the expectation to fall sleep without milk or soothing, sleep, they will not.

"I actually tried sleep training," the bouncing slows a little.

"My friends say she's too sensitive and I should try again," the bouncing stops.

"They say it worked for them," the mom sitting across from me looks down, and her voice cracks a little, "But it didn't go well for us."

Day after day, week after week, I hear this same story. I hear about sleep training being pitched as an *answer* to sensitivity and sleep, only for the experience to go awry. In many instances, even the *idea* of sensitivity is minimized, disregarded, or mistrusted.

"Those aren't real tears."

"She's just putting it on."

"She's got everything she needs, let her cry it out."

This is what we're told, by adults raised in a culture that tends to only recognize needs that we can see or measure. A dirty diaper is changed without question, yet alertness or overstimulation at bedtime after a hectic day is to be downplayed, dismissed, or disbelieved.

And importantly, we cannot measure sensitivity.

Sensitivity exists in the grey, mushy areas of life. Much like parenting in general, there is nuance and no one-size-fits-all rationale. Yet, while we cannot draw up generic rules about sensitivity and sleep, we can state with confidence that sleep training often doesn't "go well," *especially* for highly sensitive babies.

Because sleep training is not the "answer" to high sensitivity; we cannot train away genetics. We can sometimes, though not always, train away the expression of a trait, but such social conditioning carries a steep cost, since the body is intelligent enough to allow what's been pushed away and squashed down to show up in potentially less favorable and less safe ways over time. And so, importantly, we should not try to train away or "fix" sensitivity. It is not a disorder, a sign of brokenness, or a negative trait, after all.

What we *can* do, though, is work *with* our little ones' sensitivity when supporting their sleep. Understanding and working with biology creates far more ease (and sleep consolidation) than any attempt at changing or dismissing genetics.

Because a highly sensitive nervous system is exactly that: sensitive.

So, it makes sense to set a felt sense of safety as the number one priority for our sensitive babies at sleep times. By giving a highly attuned and reactive nervous system less to react and respond to, true rest can occur. This is the kind of rest that comes with a big sigh of surrender, when the internal "alarm system" isn't activated, when the external input is just right, and when sleep itself feels like a truly safe state to enter and exist within.

In moments like this we're reminded, maybe the stars can align, after all.

■ ■ ■

You are sitting on the floor, in a circle, beating a drum.

On either side of you are mothers, fathers, grandmas, babies, and toddlers, all seemingly enjoying their music class.

The other babies and toddlers clap, bang, and squeal to the beat, while the adults form a ring around them, far enough away to avoid getting struck by a drumstick.

But not you and your daughter.

You are within range of flying sticks, while your daughter is sitting on your lap, shielded from any potential impact. She presses her cheek to your chest, her wide eyes peering out from behind her curls. She is not banging the drum she was offered, so you bang it instead. You are, as always, the only adult drummer in the circle.

"My eldest was difficult like this," a voice cuts through the noise.

"Oh?" You turn and smile politely at a mom sitting a distance away from a cheerful girl dressed head to toe in yellow. The word *difficult* has somehow set you on edge.

"Yeah, she'd never join in like this one does," the mom gestures toward her sunshine-clad daughter, "She's the easiest kid! So outgoing and sleeps like a dream too!"

You smile again, of course, and return to banging your child-sized drum. Only this time, you bang a little louder, just to cut through the noise.

■ ■ ■

A mom at the park pushes her toddler on the swing, while her baby cries in the carrier. The mom sways from side to side and taps her baby's back to try to quell the fussiness.

"She skipped a nap," the mom explains, though nobody nearby is expecting or needing any kind of reasoning; most of us have been there or are there still.

"And," the mom pauses briefly, "she's not exactly an easy baby."

"Eeeezy bayyybeee!" The happily swinging toddler echoes, and everyone close by laughs, except, of course, for the baby.

There's no doubt that we've been sharing about out babies' quirks, traits, and "easiness" with other mothers in playgrounds since playgrounds were first dreamt up, and before that, these same discussions would have happened at community meeting places, in homes, and churches alike.

We are compelled to share and to ask, *is my baby like the others?*

And when the answer is, inevitably, *not quite*, we're often driven to want to understand the differences on a deeper level. Academia, too, has long focused on this idea of temperamental nuance, seeking to categorize such differences between individual babies to better understand why humans behave and develop the way we do.

Midway through the last century, researchers undertook what would become a landmark study,[51] which identified three primary "types" of temperament used to describe the general behavior and emotional patterns observed in young children and infants. Three types of temperament were identified: easy, difficult, and slow to warm up. You're not alone if you're thinking that these labels could just have easily been created at the playground, because the language used to name each one is the same language that we often hear at the swings, by the sandpit, or even in a music class.

Babies with "easy" temperaments were said to be generally adaptive and positive. They followed regular, predictable routines and patterns of behavior and recovered quickly from upset. Because of this relative "ease," sleep was seen to be unproblematic for families of babies with easy temperaments.

"Difficult" temperaments, meanwhile, were marked by irregularity and intense reactions. Babies with "difficult" temperaments took longer to adapt to change and reacted more intensely, and more negatively, to new situations. These babies tended to have irregular sleeping patterns.

Babies who were labelled as "slow to warm up" typically showed caution in new environments and appeared withdrawn or "shy." These babies did not experience the same levels of intensity or irregularity as the babies categorized as "difficult," yet they still required adequate time to adjust to new routines.

Each of these three temperament types offered researchers a framework for understanding the different ways in which children interact with their environment and how significant innate, genetically determined traits are when it comes to supporting a baby's daily rhythms and sleep.

Because a baby with a naturally programmed "easy" temperament is more likely to settle easily and sleep for longer stretches than a baby with a biologically determined "difficult" temperament— not because the parents of the "easy" baby are *doing it better*, but because their child is genetically hard-wired to adapt more seamlessly to the expectations and schedules of modern family life.

"Eeeezy bayyybeee!" The swinging toddler calls again.

"I sure wish," sighs his mom, while his little sister continues to fight the nap that's been looming with all her might.

When we talk about temperament in terms of these predefined categories, it can feel disheartening to hear about a formal labelling of infant "ease" or "difficulty," especially when we're juggling our own less-than-sunny baby or chasing nap time with every ounce of energy we have left. Yet, again, there is nuance here, and the nuance can be better understood via the concept of "goodness of fit."[52]

Goodness of fit speaks to the interplay between a baby's innate temperament and their environment. Temperament refers to the biological differences in reactivity and regulation observable in babies, while environment speaks to the immediate settings that little ones exist within, including their social contexts and the behaviors and expectations of their caregivers. Overall, babies thrive when there is a *harmonious relationship* between these puzzle pieces, even those babies who haven't been labelled as "easy."

That is, a baby who might be considered to have a "difficult" or "slow to warm up" temperament can still *thrive* in an environment that understands, respects, and meets her needs. Specifically, a baby who fights a nap schedule, and protests any new or unfamiliar comfort or soothing style for settling, can still nap easefully. This might require a flexible schedule and an empathetic caregiver, but restorative and peaceful sleep is very much still attainable. Likewise, a baby who might be deemed "slow to warm up" can still adjust her sleep patterns in alignment with her unique development trajectory. Perhaps a nap drop is imminent; this transition may require a little more time to allow for the adjustment to the new rhythm and routine, but a healthy adjustment can still occur.

"It feels like I'm dancing between both of their schedules some days," the mom at the playground is awash with relief, as her daughter is finally napping in the carrier.

It feels like I'm dancing.

This. This is exactly it.

As caregivers, we are constantly engaged in a dance between honoring our babies' innate functioning and supporting their existence in the wider world. Again, we are the bridge, the facilitators, and we facilitate *best* when we *lean in* and get to know the inner workings of the child in front of us. Because there is no singular, generic "right way" to meet the needs of every baby; nor are every baby's needs the same.

So instead, we dance.

We dance our way through the grey areas, and we try to find the best fitting environments for our little ones. This doesn't have to be perfect, either, but a well-aligned environment results in a good fit. And no matter baby's overall temperament, a good fit, not an *eeeezy bayyybeee*, is the aim.

■　■　■

You are woken in the night to your baby's cry.

You check the clock; 1:30 a.m. This is the second time you've been called tonight. You pull back the covers and reach toward the bassinet that's positioned next to your bed, scooping your little one up and into your arms.

In the dimly lit glow, you hold your baby close and sway from side to side, while your hand makes circles on her back.

Round and round, as if on autopilot, the warmth and motion of your hand soothes your daughter and she settles quickly, yet you continue to sway and make circles until she falls into a deeper sleep.

It can feel like a lot, at times, to be swaying and drawing circles like this, at 1:30 a.m.

You think of nights now past, in which you've tried other ways of soothing her. You've tried waiting a moment to see if she would settle herself. She wouldn't. You've tried holding her hand to see if she would settle without being picked up. She wouldn't. You've tried holding her in your arms, without the swaying and without the circles, but her wide eyes only grew larger and more expectant, as she waited for the to and fro, round and round soothing to begin again.

It can feel like a lot, for sure, but it works for your girl. And maybe, thankfully really, it's a good thing that you know what works, even if it's not what works for everyone.

Because maybe, thankfully really, your girl isn't like the others.

■ ■ ■

"She just needs so much, you know?"

I know.

"It's like she's looked at the catalogue of *How to Soothe Babies*, and she's gone ahead and added every single option to her wish list!"

The sweet little wisher in question grins and shouts out, at full volume, "Mama!"

"Oh, and she's loud, you know?!"

I know.

Some babies seem to need *more* than others. More movement, more noise, more sensory input overall. Each of us, as unique human beings, process our surroundings differently, after all.

These differences may be subtle, but they are there, and in addition to these differences in how we process and organize information, we also have preferences, both conscious and subconscious, as to the levels of sensory information or "input" that we feel most secure with.

When we receive information via our senses, including touch, taste, smell, sight, hearing, balance, and body awareness, we then *integrate* this information to make better sense of the world around us. This is referred to as sensory processing, and it's a functionality that helps us to respond appropriately to our ever-changing environment in a meaningful way.

It can help to imagine a pendulum swinging between very high levels of sensory input and very low levels, with individuals of all ages finding their best-fitting placement at different points along the pendulum's pathway. For our little ones, some babies will teeter toward the top of the pendulum's swing, preferring more sensory input via loud sounds, intense tastes and physical activities that provide strong vestibular or proprioceptive feedback. These little ones often seek out intense sensory input, and because of this, they can often be referred to as "sensory seekers." On the other end of the pendulum's swing, meanwhile, are babies dubbed as "sensory avoiders," who prefer reduced or minimized sensory input. In day-to-day life, sensory avoidance may present in the form of covering ears from loud noises, being "picky" with certain tastes, textures, or even clothing, and feeling most regulated in calmer environments.

We all exist at different points on this spectrum of how we process our surroundings and the level of sensory input that we function best with.[53,54,55] And importantly, neither sensory-seeking nor sensory-avoiding tendencies are classified as better or worse than the other. Within this normative swing of the sensory pendulum, the key is not to attempt to shuffle all babies into the "center," but to work with the preferences and needs of the child in front of us to understand and support their unique sensory processing preferences and integration.

"She just needs so much," my friend repeats, "And I tried the whole drowsy-but-awake thing, but she howled, you know?"

I know.

My friend birthed a sensory-seeking baby. Her daughter seeks and rests in a relatively high degree of sensory information, be it through sounds, movement, or tactile input (touch). With high levels of input, my friend's baby settles and sleeps, yet without it, sleep is a no-go.

This, right here, is just one of the reasons why the idea of setting babies down in their cribs *drowsy but awake* can often bring more stress than relief for families. Because very few babies have the sensitivity, temperament, and sensory profile necessary to allow them to feel truly secure without active, external soothing being offered at sleep times. And so, if you have also birthed a sensory-seeking baby, the stillness of the crib, the quietness of the room, and the lack of tactile input is likely to result in a swift and automatic switch away from drowsy, and straight back to fully awake.

Because it is normal for babies to fall asleep with active soothing, no matter where they land on the sensory pendulum's trajectory. Healthy sleep, after all, is an inherently vulnerable state to enter. It may feel as though the stars have to align for our babies to settle and snooze, but this celestial alignment is actually the regulation of a myriad of biological systems and functions within the body. When we feel safe, we can surrender to sleep, so the real question is, *how can I support my baby's felt sense of safety at sleep times?*

For most babies, the easiest and best fitting answer to this question is *nurture*. Nurture, through responsive caregiving and closeness, supports a baby's parasympathetic nervous system, digestive system, heart rate, breathing, and more. It also positively affects the physiological systems underlying stress responses and further relieves stress by downregulating cortisol secretion.[56] Active soothing *resets* a baby's body after a busy day and creates a truly integrated sense of safety, which leads to easier, healthier, and *better* sleep.

For sensory-seeking babies, sensitive and responsive nurture may well take a more active form than the nurture that sensory-avoiding babies might prefer. Movement via rocking, bouncing, or pacing and auditory input via white noise or lullabies will likely feel soothing for baby at bedtime. Meanwhile, for sensory-avoiding babies, we tend to notice a preference for stillness over bouncing, and the use of white noise or lullabies may simply never "work" when settling. Nothing is amiss if this is the case; we're not aiming for a generic norm after all. Instead, we're aiming to support what's normal and healthy for the unique child in front of us.

Because your baby isn't like the others (and that's no bad thing).

■　■　■

It's 10 p.m. and your mind is racing after a busy day.

It's just you and your baby at home, and there is a perfect, blissful quiet surrounding you as your little one sleeps on your chest.

You breathe in.

And out.

The racing slows a little.

Outside, the sky is dark and clouded, but if you squint through the still-open blinds, you can just about make out the brightest stars through the shape-shifting gaps in the passing clouds.

You breathe in.

And out.

The racing is almost still.

You trace your baby's profile with your own finger; how is her skin so soft? She, too, breathes in, and out, and after a while, you shuffle toward the bassinet. Without hurry, you set your baby girl down for the night, stroking her cheek as she settles into her new space. You linger a while, there in the quiet, and you realize you each have all you need.

You both breathe in and out, separately yet somehow in harmony, and all the while, the stars glimmer in the clouded night sky outside.

■ ■ ■

Pause

"My baby needs the stars to align to fall asleep."

Your baby's answer: "I sleep best with my soft blanket, mama. And when the room is dark, but not pitch black. And when there's a gentle chatter coming from across the hall, but not loud voices or sudden noises. I fall asleep most easily when you rock me just so and hold my hand just right at bedtime. Being close to you is my biggest comfort of all. I'm sure grandma thinks I'm sensitive, and I really like that word, mama. It means I notice the things others might take for granted. I feel my feelings deeply, mama, so I notice how you care for me, and I feel your love all the way down to my bones. There are some things I notice that I don't like so much, though, and in those moments, I call out to you right away. You always make it better, because you always seem to know just what to do and just what I need, too. I heard grandma say I'm a little fussy, mama, but she said it with soft eyes as she held me gently and smiled, so I don't mind, really. . .maybe I'm easy-going after all."

Prompt: How would you describe your little one's sleep personality?

Rest Assured, a Nurturing Approach

When we reframe the way in which we view sensitivity, temperament, and sensory preferences, it becomes *so much easier* to support our babies' sleep.

Why?

Because we can begin to shed the cultural narrative that casts sensitivity, fussiness, or "neediness" in a negative light.

Instead, when we accept, honor, and work with our little ones' unique needs and traits, we can use them as signposts, guiding us toward the easiest and most aligned route to sleep.

Their sensitivity becomes a cheat sheet, letting us know which soothing styles work best.

Their temperament offers an answer card to help us understand personality differences and sleep patterns in an unbiased, logical, and accepting way.

Their sensory preferences act as a map, directing us toward the environments and stimuli that best support their rest.

By working with what biology has given us, we can create flexible, family-specific rhythms and routines that support easier, more restful sleep.

Working With Sensitivity and Temperament to Support Sleep

To support our babies' sleep sensitively, we must understand and respect the unique temperament and sensitivity profile of the child in front of us.

While temperament and sensitivity are genetically determined, the interplay between a child's innate predisposition and their external environment plays a powerful role in shaping sleep patterns.

(continued)

We can support this "goodness of fit" in several ways:

- **Caregiver alignment:** Understanding and adapting to baby's temperament is likely to create a smoother sleep experience for everyone. When a parent and child have vastly different sensitivities or temperaments, needs and behaviors can be difficult to interpret. By allowing for difference and consciously working toward alignment, we can support temperamental compatibility within the family unit and foster a more fluid transition to sleep.
- **Environmental fit:** The way that a child processes their immediate environment has a direct impact on their sleep, and little ones with more sensitively wired nervous systems are likely to rest more easily, and sleep for longer stretches, in an environment that soothes rather than stimulates.
- **Predictability:** Sensitive children often thrive with consistency and routine, especially around sleep. A predictable bedtime routine can act as a *signpost* toward sleep, reducing stress by creating familiarity and security.
- **Sensory input:** Sleep onset can be supported or halted by the sensory input a child is exposed to. Understanding your child's unique sensory needs can help shape an approach that works best for them.

Does Your Baby Need Down-Regulation Up-Regulation Before Sleep?

Some babies need a period of calm before bed (down-regulation), while others need physical input (up-regulation) to transition to sleep smoothly.

- Babies who need down-regulation often settle best with:
  - Calm, quiet voices
  - Dim lighting
  - Stillness before sleep

- Babies who need up-regulation tend to benefit from:
  - Movement, such as rocking or swaying
  - Deep pressure input, via cuddles or holding
  - Tactile input, via fiddling or stroking different textures
  - Oral input, via feeding or pacifier use

By observing, responding, and matching baby's unique needs consistently, we can create a predictable, secure sleep environment, which, in turn, supports better rest.

Is Your Baby Highly Sensitive?

Highly sensitive babies tend to:

- Take longer to fall asleep after a busy day
- Have big reactions to sensory stimuli (such as labels in clothes, loud hand dryers in public bathrooms, or certain food textures)
- Be slow to warm up to new situations and caregivers
- Resist sleep in bright, busy environments
- Notice and respond deeply to a caregiver's mood
- Startle easily at sudden or loud noises
- Be highly aware of and tuned into their surroundings
- Take longer to settle into a rhythm during vacation or after an illness
- Be prone to frustration or intense meltdowns

What's Your Baby's Temperament?

- **Easy temperament:** Predictable sleep patterns, quick adaptability to change, and calm, cheerful moods. These babies tend to fall into natural sleep rhythms with minimal support.
- **Difficult temperament:** Irregular sleep–wake cycles, intense emotional responses, and a strong reaction to

(continued)

changes in routine or environment. These babies may have a harder time settling and often require extra patience and consistency in sleep routines.

♦ **Slow-to-warm-up temperament:** Cautious about new experiences, withdraws in unfamiliar settings, and may need extra time to adjust to transitions. These babies often need predictability and reassurance to feel secure at bedtime.

What's Your Baby's Sensory Profile?

♦ Sensory-seeking babies often:
  • Settle to sleep with movement, such as rocking, pacing, or swaying
  • Fidget and fiddle with objects or certain textiles or fabrics
  • Sleep best in close physical contact with a caregiver
  • Seek proprioceptive input, such as massage or tight cuddles
  • Seek vestibular input, such as spinning or swinging
♦ Sensory-avoiding babies often:
  • Resist motion at sleep times
  • Prefer stillness when falling asleep
  • Sleep best in an independent sleep space
  • Avoid proprioceptive input
  • Are more cautious of vestibular input

CHAPTER 9

Everything Changes

"How old is he?"

You're at the grocery store and the mom standing behind you in line tilts her head toward your baby.

"Oh, he's just coming up to four months," you smile and take a step forward as the line shortens.

"Uh oh, four months, are you ready for the dreaded sleep regression?!"

You stare, blankly, and take another step forward.

"It almost took us out, I swear!" The mom laughs and pushes her toddler's stroller another inch or two, as the line moves again.

It's your turn, finally. You're thankful there's no need to think of a reply but simultaneously wrestling with the discomfort that's starting to crawl through your body.

When you get back to your car, baby and bags loaded and ready to go, you pause for a moment before starting the engine, and type four words into your phone:

Four month sleep regression.

There, in the palm of your hand, you're supplied with article after article, blog post after blog post, about the horrors of baby sleep at four months.

Increased night waking.

A permanent change to how your baby sleeps.

More fussing.

Less napping.

Trouble falling asleep.

A sudden worsening of sleep.

Page after page, words of doom stare back at you, alongside discussion threads from forums where every post submitted by a parent of a four-month-old baby seems to begin with one word:

Help.

From the back seat, your baby boy begins to whimper, so you put your phone away, start the engine, and begin your journey back home. It's not long before the whimpers fade away and sleep overtakes your son, so you drive the rest of the way home in silence. Yet one word in particular won't stop looping inside your brain:

Help, help, help.

■ ■ ■

At four months, sleep changes, and it does so at a structural level.

Before babies are born, and in the initial months post birth, their sleep architecture is inherently immature, with sleep cycling between just two stages of sleep: active sleep and quiet sleep. During active sleep, which is crucial for brain development and the processing of sensory information, babies tend to smile and grimace. This stage is characterized by rapid eye movements (REMs), irregular breathing, and increased brain activity. In quiet sleep, meanwhile, which promotes physical growth and cellular repair, babies tend to be less responsive to external stimuli, and relatively still. This is the stage in which babies often seem to be oblivious to their external environment, sleeping through the afternoon, for instance, even when the house is filled with visitors, sunlight, and noise.

At around four months, though, things start to change due to a peak in development that alters infant sleep architecture to include *more* sleep stages, mirroring adult sleep, albeit loosely. This is the point in time where many families panic.

"It's the dreaded four-month sleep regression!" My friend's voice echoes through the phone.

"Progression," I offer.

"Pro? Progression? Louise, what the. . ."

I know, I really do.

When we're in it, it doesn't feel like progress at all.

For the "lucky" ones, with sleepy newborns who settle easily and sleep for long stretches of several hours at a time, the shock that the four-month development leap can bring in terms of its potential impact on sleep is intense. And for those of us who birthed super-sensitive, super-alert, super-hungry little beings, the idea of our already-fragmented nights likely getting even *more* wakeful can be a difficult pill to swallow.

You'll notice that I'm using words like "potential" and "likely" here, and it feels important to mention that not all families notice this shift and maturation of sleep cycles, which can cause more frequent wake-ups at this stage. There are in fact babies, most likely the ones coming into this world with easy temperaments, who breeze through this period without any telltale signs that this inevitable and biologically expected sleep cycle development is actively taking place. Anecdotally, I call these babies *Unicorn Babies*, and as the name suggests, Unicorn Babies are rare. *Most* babies are not unicorns and will experience a patch of "wobbly" sleep at around four months of age, with more wakefulness as they navigate this leap. The key here for parents is to remember that we have not caused the wobble. Not with our soothing. Not with our comforting. Not with our middle-of-the-night need-meeting. It's biology that's driving every extra wake, every extra feed, and every extra-long bedtime, and when we frame development as the biological phenomenon that it is, it becomes so much easier to reconcile any wobbles that we might be experiencing.

So, what's causing the wobble?

Gone are the newborn days, where babies moved through just two sleep stages. Now, infant sleep cycles are beginning to look much more adult-like, cycling through various stages of non-rapid eye movement (NREM) sleep and one stage of REM sleep. Within this new and matured multistage cycling, we see important and necessary biological developments, facilitated exclusively via this more complex sleep patterning, or architecture.

In stage one of a baby's newly matured sleep cycle, little ones transition from wakefulness to sleep. This is the entry point, or gateway, to sleep, and offering soothing during this stage can be especially helpful for supporting babies to fall asleep easily and with low stress markers. In stage two, often referred to as "true sleep," sleep deepens to support neural cognition and memory consolidation. Stages three and four are often combined and referred to as "deep sleep." Deep sleep is important for physical restoration, growth hormone release, and immune function. The final stage of each sleep cycle is REM sleep, which supports brain development and emotional processing.

Each and every stage of a baby's sleep cycle has a positive biological function, essential for growth and healthy development. This is an important note, because we are often told, "Only deep sleep counts!" Deep sleep counts, of course, but so do the other stages of sleep. To attempt to rush, remove, or devalue any individual stage undermines what the cycle as a whole is actually *doing*: supporting our babies' thriving. And so, this four-month shift toward more complexity within each cycle allows sleep to develop appropriately and function optimally. If this natural progression wasn't so challenging for families to navigate, there's a good chance that it would be celebrated, instead of outright feared.

"Shouldn't a progression feel, I don't know, progressive?!"

My friend is unimpressed and speaking the thoughts that most of us have had as we wrestle with the sleep disruptions that can peak at this age and stage. Yet the truth is, some progress is invisible. Some progress masks as discomfort or unpredictability. Some progress happens incrementally and takes a wholly nonlinear route. Yet progress it is, nonetheless.

This progressive restructuring of sleep is unique at the four-month mark. Because this age and stage signifies a *true sleep progression*, from immature to more complex sleep patterning, facilitating more time spent in lighter stages of sleep. This is the only leap that instigates a direct alteration in sleep architecture. That is, every other development leap or peak that our babies experience can be considered a developmental progression, as opposed to a sleep progression.

"It just feels like we're moving backwards as opposed to forwards," my friend sighs, "But I suppose progress isn't always obvious, right?"

Right.

Exactly right, in fact, because sometimes, progress only looks like progress when we zoom out.

■ ■ ■

"Zoom in!"

Your sister is calling to you as she holds out her arms for your baby to step-fall into.

"Get a close up, this is too cute!"

You're hovering a distance away, recording these first, wobbly steps on your phone, eyes brimming with pride.

Wasn't he brand new, just yesterday?

One, two, three steps are taken before your sister scoop-swirls your baby boy up and into the air, triumphant.

The three of you dance in celebration of this huge, magnificent feat. First steps. It's a landmark occasion that calls for milk, and a nap.

A little while later, as your little one snoozes, you push him in his stroller and walk beside your sister.

"I *knew* it was coming," you explain, "He's been trying *so* hard to walk lately!"

You weave the stroller between two puddles but end up stepping in one yourself.

"And it's like he's forgotten how to sleep," you continue, unphased by your now soppy puddle-foot, "I think that's normal when they're learning stuff, though, right?"

Your sister shrugs.

"I mean, it makes sense," she offers, "His brain must be working hard because walking isn't as easy as it looks, is it?"

She cackles as your other foot splashes through another would-be-avoidable puddle, and all the while, your baby snoozes on.

■ ■ ■

When we're deep in the daily and nightly graft of these early years, it can feel like sleep takes a step backward, or "regresses," in alignment with, and caused by, every single peak in development. Yet, with the exception of the four-month leap, the foundations of infant sleep architecture are not technically changing with each and every leap.

That is, after sleep cycles alter to become more complex at four months, the developmental changes we witness with sleep are less acute. Shifts such as a lengthening of each cycle's duration, and an overall decrease in the number of hours spent awake each day, can feel steadier. In real terms, these shifts tend to result in dropped naps, later bedtimes, and for some, earlier mornings as sleep needs lessen and little ones grow to be able to stay awake, happily and healthily, for longer stretches at once. And yet, many parents will report that sleep begins to wobble at every single leap, or peak, in development throughout the early years.

This consensus is so well accepted that the language we commonly use to discuss these peaks in development tends to focus solely on sleep.

The six-month sleep regression.
The eight-month sleep regression.
The twelve-month sleep regression.

These time stamps of infancy are not markers of regressing sleep architecture. They are, instead, markers of developmental progressions and, as such, are more accurately referred to as development leaps (or peaks). Yet at each of these leaps, it's common for sleep to become wobbly all over again, which raises the question, *what's causing these particular wobbles?*

The biology behind developmental sleep wobbles is multifaceted. Firstly, growth and development are calorie-intensive activities. Physically, our babies require a frequent supply of energy to fuel their growing bodies. Frequent feeds act to facilitate a steady supply of calories, to meet a baby's energy requirements, no matter the time of day (or night).

Adjacent to the need for continuing calories, is the need for comfort and specifically, biological regulation. Because when we feel safe, truly deeply safe, our bodies become very efficient at utilizing the energy that we're taking in. A stressed baby will actively seek regulation, while a comforted baby already rests within it. Through comfort and soothing, vital energy isn't spent on seeking safety, because internal safety markers are already checked off. This allows for the body to grow, to restore, and to develop as it needs to, which, in turn, creates an internal safety loop, whereby safety results in regulation, which results in safety, and on and on.

During peaks in development, where more energy is required to facilitate growth, extra wake-ups and a higher drive toward proximity and soothing just make sense. Yet, development doesn't always result in an outgrown onesie; it's not simply a peak in calorie consumption and musculoskeletal growth that babies are experiencing regularly during these early, formative years; they're also experiencing peaks in neurological development and skill acquisition, too.

This is the very definition of progress, not regression.

Because our little ones are moving forward, not backward. They are learning and integrating their experiences and skills faster than they ever will again, with more than one million connections formed every second within the infant brain.[57] We can think of these wobbly patches of sleep as markers of intense brain development.

"He was waking all night! Completely out of nowhere," my friend laughs and shakes her head, relieved to be through the wobble.

"But then he wakes one morning and in the sweetest voice, he whispers, "*Mama*," she smiles, "I swear I melted right there."

Our babies' brains are working hard, so hard, and while some of the skills that they're integrating are obvious, such as crawling or walking, others, such as figuring out social cues or language acquisition, are far more covert. Some skills will show up out of nowhere and take us by surprise, while others may give us forewarnings, if we're paying close attention, as we can sometimes recognize the next skill that's about to be attained ahead of time.

"I should have known, to be fair," my friend reflected.

"He'd been nonstop babbling at 2 a.m. for the last week," she pauses, "Practice makes perfect!"

Skill acquisition requires practice.

At any age and stage, practice is what acts to integrate learning and "protect" the neural networks behind it. We "use it or lose it" when it comes to our brain connections, remember? And for our babies, their practice sessions often crop up at night, when their bodies are resting and their brains are busy "wiring" and integrating the experiences and learning they've been working hard on all day. These wobbles, then, can be thought of as a "side effect" of biologically healthy and appropriate development. Rather than a sleep problem in need of a fix, more frequent waking during developmental leaps is a normal feature of a healthy infancy.

We see pre-crawling babies moving around more in their cribs, before they begin to crawl, just as we see pre-verbal babies vocalizing at 2 a.m., before they utter their first words. It's fascinating to witness this positioning of their "real-world learning" with their internal neural integration, together with their external practicing of the new skill. It's another biological "dance," with nuanced and often-invisible steps that support learning to move our little ones forward in their development, the truest marker of progress amid this season of inherent change.

■　■　■

You are walking through the store when you hear someone calling your name.

Not "Mom" or "Mommy" or "Mama."

Your actual name.

You turn to see a smartly dressed woman making her way toward you.

"It's been so long!" She chimes, "And who is this little one? How precious!"

She's smiling at your baby, asleep in the carrier, and you notice your heartbeat pick up the pace, just a tad.

You have no idea who this friendly woman is. There is no area of your brain that can recall her face or ever having met her before. Yet she knows you, clearly.

"Just out for a few bits, are we?" She breezes on, gesturing to your empty cart.

"Oh, yeah, I just came for. . .," your voice trails away.

You've forgotten. You have no recollection of the human in front of you or the items you set out to buy from the store.

You smile your biggest smile, throw in a couple of nice-to-see-you comments, and one or two we-should-catch-up-for-coffee-sometime comments, and then you're on your way.

You're sweating, but you survived.

The drama has woken your baby boy from his dreaming, and he's squirming in the carrier, making you sweat even more profusely. You curse the postpartum hormones for their insistence on excessive leaking, throw a few basics into your cart, and make a dash toward the checkout.

It's only when you're finally back at home that you realize you forgot the milk.

■　■　■

"Mommy brain" knows no bounds; but what exactly is happening to our brains, postpartum?

In the simplest of terms, mommy brain is a sign of a deeper biological shift that happens when we become mothers. And yet, there tends to be very limited information or support made available to new mothers, regarding what changes to expect *for themselves*, post birth.

The development that we witness in our babies after birth is expected. We watch our newborns become babies, our babies become toddlers, our toddlers become preschoolers, and so on. We pack away outgrown onesies and baby booties with a sometimes-heavy acceptance that such growth and change is what we signed up for.

Yet for mothers, information about *maternal development* post birth is rarely discussed and largely inaccessible, which is a problem. Because we undergo monumental shifts as we enter and exist within motherhood. In body, mind, and soul, we are birthed anew, too.

Something that's barely ever mentioned, and often misunderstood, is the fact that the postpartum maternal brain changes with motherhood, much akin to a neurological "reorganization." We see a "pruning" of the neural pathways that do not serve us best in this new season, which essentially roots back (as most biology does) to the idea of safety. Not safety for ourselves as individual humans, though: safety for the babies we have birthed.

Because mothers and infants are a dyadic unit.

Our babies' biology is still interconnected with our own.

Our instincts are no longer self-serving, but self-and-child-serving.

Much like a "mama bear" who is innately and fiercely protective of her cubs, new mothers are biologically wired to protect our young. This neurological reorganization of the maternal brain explains the biology behind why mothers seem to have innate superhuman strength, intuition, and reactions yet can't always recall an acquaintance's name or remember to buy milk at the store. Our brains are pruning away the less important neural pathways while safeguarding and fine-tuning the most important ones. We lose what doesn't serve us anymore to make space and protect what serves our new role best. It's a true "both, and" phenomenon, both a loss and a gain, which speaks to the nuances and grey areas of motherhood in general.

Because motherhood can feel both beautiful, and messy.

It can feel both soul-giving, and exhausting.

It can feel, at times, both easeful, and simultaneously complex.

As mothers, we live in the messy middle, where two truths can and do co-exist at once. Aspects of our functioning may seem to "regress," yet our most crucial skills become supercharged. We are tailoring our skills for efficiency and effectiveness at the huge task and ask of raising babies. And so, it makes sense that change is not reserved purely for our little ones. We undergo immense changes too, with reorganized, better-prioritized brains, and this creates a ripple effect of other, related changes that we may or may not notice day-to-day.

When our internal "mama bear" is alerted, it's fiercely apparent, and so is the social awkwardness of blanking on people's names. There are certain changes, though, which arrive quietly and are rarely noticed, yet these changes still serve us in the most powerful ways. One such change is how we sleep, as mothers, postpartum.

"The doctor asked if I'm getting my eight hours," my friend's voice is wavering between exasperation and hilarity.

"My eight hours," she continues, "as if I'm sleeping eight hours straight right now!"

Hilarity wins, just, and she laughs the slightly wild laugh of someone who is all-too-familiar with middle-of-the-night wake-ups.

Let's run through the slightly wild logic of postpartum sleep, shall we?

We grow and birth immature, entirely dependent beings that steal our hearts with their gurgles and skin folds. We are tasked with the job of keeping these little beings safe so that they can thrive, and part of that safekeeping is to ensure that they are nourished and nurtured, day and night. And so, we tend to them; we feed them, hold them, rock them, and whisper to them, day and night. Long gone are the days where we went to bed in the evening, slept, and woke for the day in the morning. Now, we follow a different rhythm: one that flows between sleeping and waking, sleeping and waking, the whole night through. This makes sense for baby, biologically speaking, because such need-meeting facilitates the safekeeping that's so important. Yet en masse, we assume that every mother is set up to suffer with such disruption to her sleep. We are told that a generic eight hours of continual sleep is the goal for all adults, without exception. We are judged, or perhaps worse, pitied for our nighttime nurturing.

"Eight hours straight," my friend is recovering from the hilarity, "I don't get all eight," she shrugs, "But I figure I'm getting enough."

How can this be? How can millions of mothers be functioning and healthy without a continuous eight hours of sleep each night? Again, biology has the answer.

Firstly, maternal physiology alters dramatically after birth. Oxytocin, our "love" hormone, increases in both baby *and mom* during breastfeeds and during acts that promote physical proximity, such as holding our little ones close while offering a bottle. When oxytocin spikes, feelings of sleepiness are common, which helps babies to fall asleep, of course, but this also supports *an easier return to sleep for mom* after a nighttime wake up or feed.

Prolactin, meanwhile, which is our "milk-making" hormone, rises during pregnancy and remains high during lactation. Prolactin doesn't only promote milk production, though; it also offers *protection* against sleep disturbances, by altering maternal sleep architecture.[58,59,60,61,62] At one month postpartum, we see new mothers spending *less* time in the first and second stages of each sleep cycle and significantly *more* time in sleep stage three. Stage three is slow-wave, or "deep sleep," which supports restoration, growth, and immune function. Our postpartum hormonal profile alters to better optimize and prioritize our recovery and health.

Aside from the postpartum hormonal shifts that are occurring, there is also development occurring in terms of a new mother's connection with her new baby. We see heightened attunement, with mom's ability to sensitively adjust and respond to her baby's signals amplified thanks to her newly altered postpartum hormonal profile and newly organized, or *prioritized*, "mommy brain." We also see a mirroring or "matching" of behaviors, emotional states, and biological rhythms.[63] Specifically, sleep synchrony between a mother and her child in the postpartum period allows for an alignment of maternal and infant sleep patterns, with infant awakenings typically synchronizing with the lighter stages of mom's sleep cycle.[64] Such synchronization is one of the reasons why proximity at sleep times during the early months is recommended, since exposure to mom's cues such as body heat, heartbeat, and even breathing patterns has been found to reduce baby's risk of SIDS and positively influence the synchronization of maternal–infant sleep patterning.[65,66]

"Don't get me wrong," my friend has stopped laughing, "I am tired. Like, tired to my bones. I just have to remind myself that it's not forever."

Even when we can explain the altered sleep, our lived experience of nighttime nurturing can often leave us feeling tired. Tired to our bones, in fact. Much of this relates back to the culture and era that we're mothering within. We are all, each and every one of us, at the mercy of a larger social system. And that social system was not designed with nighttime nurturing in mind. When we live in nuclear family units, many miles from extended family, with bills to pay, jobs outside of the home, jobs inside of the home, multiple children, and a million other responsibilities, it becomes startlingly apparent just how difficult it is to flow with baby's needs while also meeting our own.

Because a 2 a.m. feed feels acutely disruptive when the alarm is set for 6 a.m. And a skipped nap feels acutely disappointing when it was the only time we had set aside to rest. It is hard, in every sense, to function well in a world that demands so much of us while simultaneously balancing the needs of a baby whose biology is effectively thousands of years old. We cannot typically "sleep when the baby sleeps," though if this option presents itself to you, I encourage you to grab it with both hands, without hesitation.

Plus, and this is so often overlooked; there are many reasons for maternal exhaustion that are not directly related to how baby is, or isn't, sleeping. Specifically, while postpartum fatigue is, of course, linked to reduced sleep time, it is also closely associated with conditions such as low hemoglobin levels, low ferritin levels,[67] anemia, endometritis, urinary tract infections, mastitis, and thyroid dysfunction, all of which are considered risks for new mothers.[68]

Because everything changes for us as moms, postpartum, including our health risk profiles, the number of hours sleep we're logging, and how we're biologically functioning to cope and hopefully thrive through it all.

■ ■ ■

It's 6 a.m., and a hand is tapping your face.

Pulled from sleep, you open your blurry eyes and focus on the gummy smile hovering close.

Your baby's day has begun, as it always does, with nothing but delight at seeing your sleepy face.

Even with your bedhead, milk-stained pajamas, and sleepiness, you are, without question, his everything.

You pull him close for a cuddle, and he settles in, not sleepy but peacefully enjoying the closeness. He is warm and smells like sleep. You close your eyes again and breathe him in, just as he is in this moment.

It won't always be like this, you know.

Some days, that simple truth brings relief. The idea that one day in the future you'll have your nights back feels like hope. You look forward to a time with easier car rides and days that don't revolve around naps. You can almost taste the sweetness of freedom that will come with the next season of motherhood, and the next after that.

But not this morning.

This morning, you breathe in the softness and warmth of your baby and wish that you could package this moment up to keep forevermore. This morning, you hold him close and pray for the minutes to stretch, just enough to savor every last second.

Because this too shall pass, and everything changes, you're well aware; but for now, you're too blissfully lost in the moment to think of anything other than your baby's perfect 6 a.m. smile.

■ ■ ■

Pause

"My baby's sleep regresses with every development leap!"

Your baby's answer: "I'm learning so much, mama, and I've been working so hard on my skills. Your eyes light up when you see me crawling toward you, and honestly, there's no place else I'd want to crawl to. I know I've been waking at night quite a lot, lately. And your eyes aren't so lit up when you come to me in the darkness, though I can see that they're still soft and filled with love. Thank you for coming when I need you. It won't stay like this, mama, I promise. These days and nights will soon feel like a lifetime ago, and maybe you'll look back with lit-up eyes, or maybe they'll simply be soft with remembering and love, but either way, thank you."

Prompt: How does it feel to re-frame a sleep regression as a sleep progression?

Rest Assured, a Nurturing Approach

Sleep during developmental leaps can feel wobbly and unpredictable, so having a *Progression Toolkit* to lean on when things feel particularly rough can make a big difference.

It's doesn't need to be fancy or overly complicated; even the simplest of steps can improve our experience of these sleep-disturbing peaks in learning and development.

Because when we are supporting development, we are, by default, supporting sleep.

Progression Toolkit

◆ **Support baby's sleep drives:** Sleep is a biological function, and when we support its biological roots, it wobbles a little less during leaps. This means prioritizing outside time, movement, and connection each day.

◆ **Encourage skill practice during the day:** Developmental leaps often involve new motor and cognitive skills that require plenty of practice time. New skills integrate once they have been "tried out" and expressed time and again, so allowing for daytime practice sessions will help to reduce the likelihood of midnight rehearsals. Depending on the milestone, this might mean:

• Creating space for crawling, cruising, or walking

• Supporting language development with repetition, music, and mirroring of baby's sounds, tone, and pitch

• Using "serve and return" interactions, by pausing and waiting for baby to "reply" during conversations

◆ **Cut corners where you can:** Lowering expectations and reducing nonessential commitments can help you conserve energy and create a sense of ease during this more intense period.

◆ **Follow baby's feeding cues:** Energy requirements and expenditure fluctuate with musculoskeletal growth and development, and feeding patterns often shift during leaps. Trusting baby's hunger cues helps ensure their energy needs are met in alignment with their development.

♦ **Lean into the changes:** Babies often seek more comfort and feed more frequently during leaps. It's common to wonder if meeting these needs will create habits that are hard to change, but the truth is, met needs dissipate; they do not fester.

Giving the extra cuddle or feed is not creating a "bad habit." It's responding to a real need, and soon enough, those "extras" won't be needed, requested or offered at all.

♦ **Use the five-year rule:** One of my favorite strategies, the five-year rule, is an approach I lean on time and again, both in my own life and in my practice with clients. The concept is simple; in challenging moments, ask yourself:

Will this matter in five years' time?

Will I regret these moments, five years from now?

Reflecting in this way can help us to find solid ground during these oftentimes wobbly patches. It can give us both perspective and resolve.

Progress Isn't Always Linear

Sleep may well seem to take two steps forward and one step back, on repeat, in this season, but progress is not always linear, and nor is it always apparent.

If we look closely enough, though, perhaps when we convince ourselves that the rest of the world must be asleep while we're awake and soothing in the depths of the night, we might just catch a glimpse of it.

In the way their hair is beginning to curl.

In the way their babbles are sounding more and more like "Mama."

In the way their onesie is all-of-a-sudden too small.

Because if there's one thing that's certain in these early years, it's that *everything changes*.

CHAPTER 10

You're Not the Only One Doing It This Way

You are at the playground, pushing your daughter on the swing. She squeals with delight with every push.

Close by, a group of moms are making their way past the swing set and slide. They are pushing strollers and sipping take-out coffee, deep in conversation. There's an ease to their group, a sense of belonging that you haven't yet found as a mom, and you can't help but notice a wave of something rising deep within you.

Jealousy? No.

Loneliness? More likely.

You don't have a cluster of mom friends to grab coffee with or head out for a stroll together. You don't have anyone, in fact, who's currently navigating this same stage of life alongside you.

"I love my sleep," you catch a few words from their conversation as they get closer, and you can't help but hold your breath.

"You guys did cry it out, right?"

Heads nod in unison.

"Yeah, I think we'll start there."

You release your still-held breath, and a new wave rises.

Judgment? No.

Loneliness? More likely.

Because it seems like everyone else does sleep *differently* than you.

Your baby's squeals steal back your attention. You push her again and again, and she laughs.

Her laughter feels like balm, somehow. It's louder than the conversation you should never have been listening to, and it steadies you as the mommy group passes by.

After a while, your arms grow tired from pushing, almost as tired as the rest of your body, after another night of teething and feeds.

"Shall we head home for a nap?" You ask your baby girl as you bring the swing to a halt.

She instantly reaches her arms toward you.

"Mama," she smiles.

"Yes, nap with Mama," you scoop her up and grab your bag, pausing to kiss her cheek.

You love your sleep too, you realize. You just do it your way.

■　■　■

"Everyone I know sleep trains."

This is what I hear, time and again, and the words are often cloaked with something.

Jealousy? No.

Judgment? No.

Loneliness? More likely.

Because when it feels like *everyone else* is taking a different path, the path that we're on can feel lonely.

This path that we seem to be forging can feel *otherly* at best and outright risky at worst. We step through our days with an awareness of not quite fitting in with the status quo, and then find ourselves awake and soothing at 1 a.m., 2 a.m., or 3 a.m. with a dose of worry nestling alongside the tiredness. But it can help, so much, to know that there are others.

There are others choosing not to sleep train.

There are others contact napping with their babies.

There are others awake and soothing at 2 a.m.

Because you're not the only one doing it this way, and I can say that with certainty, since I meet families doing it your way every single day.

"Nobody understands," a mom is sitting across from me with tears in her eyes.

"Everybody, literally everybody I know, has done some kind of sleep training."

A tear traces its way down her cheek, and she quickly brushes it away. Meanwhile, her baby sleeps peacefully in her arms. In this moment, this mom is not chasing a nap or battling through a long, drawn-out bedtime. Sleep itself is not the stressor, not right now at least. I watch as her fingers swirl circles on her sleeping baby's back and notice how she pauses from time to time simply to breathe her little one in. Here in this moment, she's not being woken from a restful sleep to go and pace the nursery, babe in arms. She's not watching the clock or counting down the hours until morning. She's doing what countless generations have done before her; she's nurturing her baby and, by default, herself. Even with tears in her eyes and a lingering sense that she's the only one, she allows her child to rest in her arms and find comfort against her skin. Even with the doubts and the loneliness, she continues along the path that feels so otherly, yet is generations deep.

"I promise there are others." There is certainty in my voice as I say, "We are many."

I offer the words as reassurance, but they sound more like a rally cry.

While sleep training seems to dominate the cultural narrative around sleep, there are many, many families opting out. Even within research populations and clinical settings, "parental resistance" to sleep training as a sleep intervention has been documented for more than 30 years.[69,70,71,72,73] Researchers report high drop-out rates for families refusing to "ignore" their babies' crying, alongside "noncompliance" due to ethical concerns.[74,75,76,77,78] There is even evidence[79] that up to *three quarters* of parents either opt out of extinction-methods, such as "crying it out" or "controlled crying," or begin the process and stop soon after due to concerns that continuing would have an emotionally detrimental impact on both baby and parent. Interestingly, the parents opting out of controlled crying were said to be more likely to be *emotionally focused* on their babies, while those going ahead with the intervention were identified as being more *outcome focused*.

Outcome focused is an especially important term, because it leads to the question, how are we defining the outcome? Are we taking a close-up look at the immediate outcome, or are we zooming out and into the future? Are we viewing the outcome purely in terms of sleep, or are we considering the interconnected "puzzle pieces" of attachment, development, feeding, well-being, and so on?

To segment one aspect—sleep—and view it as an isolated component is to risk the fracture of the full puzzle. Plus, sleep training does not guarantee the immediate outcome of a full night's sleep, and the irony here is that when we do take a broader look at sleep interventions, supporting sleep through responsivity, attachment, and connection has been found to bring vast improvements to both infant sleep and parental sleep alike.[80,81,82,83,84]

That is, responding to cries, not ignoring them, brings positive outcomes in both the short-term and the long-term, and is also favored by many, many parents as a low-stress sleep intervention,[85] or, more aptly, sleep *support*.

With decades of research[86] now highlighting the significance of attachment and responsivity for raising healthy humans, we are witnessing these themes translate to the world of infant sleep in real time, and the more we look, the more we find evidence that nurture, not disconnect, is the key for supporting our babies' sleep. Not just in the long-term, either, since we are also witnessing immediate and tangible positive outcomes of responsivity in relation to sleep.

Specifically, we can now evidence the significance of maternal emotional availability, whereby higher emotional availability is associated with fewer infant night wakings.[87] We can also evidence the power of responsiveness overall, since increased parental responsiveness has been shown to result in significantly better infant sleep behaviors.[88] And attunement, too, is now evidenced as being a key factor in supporting baby sleep, with increased attunement resulting in an increase in the total time that babies spend asleep in any 24-hour window.[89]

Time and again, we witness the power of tuning in and sensitively responding to the cues and needs of the babies in our care. We now have the evidence to support the instincts that have shaped our parenting practices for thousands of years, and yet, it's still *so easy* to feel like the only one tuning in, the only one responding, and the only one opting for sleep *support* over sleep training.

What's striking is the apparent discord between the instinct-supporting data we have and the advice that parents are often given by professionals, family, friends, or the Internet in general. It takes time to change any social narrative, and sleep training via disconnect and a lack of responsiveness is deeply woven into our current cultural context. It's no surprise that "opting out" can feel like an act of rebellion.

"We are many."

I say it again, and this time, I own the battle cry. It feels powerful, and needed, to know that we aren't alone. Because there is power in community. Our ancestors knew it, for sure, and if we look closely enough, the data shows it too; the power and significance of parental support cannot be overestimated. Specifically, "active encouragement" is pinpointed and highlighted as being essential to the success of any sleep support intervention being studied.[90]

When we move beyond solely attempting to directly "fix" sleep itself and focus instead on the indirect support that's born of supporting parents and strengthening parent–child relationships, we see improved infant sleep as a natural consequence.[91,92] It's almost as if *support*, for both babies and parents alike, is key for a good night's sleep. . . .

■ ■ ■

You are in the depths of a conversation you'd rather not be having.

"And I told her," your husband's aunt leans closer, "I told her, she'll be sorry! She'll never get that kid out of their bed!"

You shuffle uncomfortably and pull your baby a little closer.

"Bed! Mama, bed!" Your baby's joy breaks the tension, but it carries its own risk.

"Shhhh," you half-joke, worried your own sleeping arrangements will be given away.

Your baby sees your bed as her own, or rather, as a shared space. The big bed is also your family bed, though not always. Sometimes, you'll fall asleep while you're settling her at bedtime, curled up together on her floor bed. Other nights, she'll spend half the night in her bed and half in yours. Rarely, the family bed wins for the whole night through. Within the walls of your home, this is no big deal. It doesn't feel significant or strange, just helpful. It helps to have the option and space to play "musical beds," as needed. Yet out here, where family and friends and strangers carry and share stories of others, laced with opinions and judgments, your sleep arrangements feel delicate, as if one side-eye or arched brow could fracture what's been working so well.

"Shhhh," you offer again, this time on autopilot and perhaps to quieten your own thoughts, but your husband's aunt has changed topics and is now discussing the marital status of a family friend.

You breathe out and zone out, simultaneously, relieved to be out of the line of fire.

■ ■ ■

"I don't know anyone else who cosleeps."

"I don't know anyone else who still offers night feeds."

"I don't know anyone else who holds their baby for naps."

This is what I'm told, over and again, and every time I hear these words, I want to connect the dots and build a bridge between families.

"Look," I want to show them, *"you're not the only one."*

Yet, there is an ever-present sense of pressure and misfitting expectations around infant sleep, which stem from a generalized "illiteracy" of infancy. That is, as a culture, we have a rather skewed perspective of what babies need and how they should sleep and develop. This altered perspective is rooted in more than a century of behaviorism, whereby parents have been firmly told that children are to be seen and not heard, with outward behavior deemed more important than inward feelings. The result? Nurture, and its related practices, has become a subculture. An underground, quiet movement that's carried out almost in secret, in the arms of mothers and in whispers of, "Mama's here," in dimly lit bedrooms during the depths of the night.

My daughter was five years old when she met Mimi. She ran out of school one day and told me about a new friend she'd met in class, so I scanned the playground for this new little girl's mom, and within 10 minutes, Mimi's mom and I were friends for life.

She told me about their move, her teaching job, and their new home. She told me about her daughters, both as they were and as they had been. Her eyes shone as she told me how Mimi would contact nap for hours at a time as a baby and climb into the big bed halfway through the night as a toddler, just to be close. She laughed as she described both of her daughters' insistence on closeness throughout their preschool years.

Every day, families share their worlds with me. Their wins and their worries, how often their little ones wake, and where their children sleep. But to have this happen out in the world, away from a professional space, served as a reminder of just how powerful community and solidarity are when we're raising our babies. And it wasn't the contact naps that connected us; it was the unapologetic truth of Mimi's mom's words. It was the way they fell from her mouth so easily, without needing to shield themselves from side-eyeing or arched brows.

Because we weren't built to do this alone. We are wired for connection and sharing, and never is such wiring more apparent than during the early years when we're brand new, too. When we're learning as we go. When we're negotiating a culture that doesn't readily offer us the insight or answers that we're so often searching for.

Wakeful baby? Sleep train.

Clingy baby? Disconnect.

Tearful baby? You're spoiling her.

This is the fabric of our culture, which tells us loud and clear: nurture is irrelevant at best, and dangerous at worst.

Remember John Watson's direction to parents, back in the 1920s? *"Never hug and kiss them."*[93]

This was the advice given to our great grandparents, which will have trickled down to our grandparents, to our parents, and now to us.

This anti-nurture directive is loud and insistent, and so, when we find ourselves postpartum, laced with nurture-fueling hormones and cradling a child that was made of our flesh and has eyes that understand our very soul, it can feel confronting. It can feel disorienting to be leaning into nurture when we exist within a cultural context that's so heavily weighted against tender, connected, and sensitive caregiving.

Nurture itself can feel otherly, just at first—until, that is, we meet another who knows what we know and feels what we feel.

Wakeful baby? Go to her.

Clingy baby? Hold her.

Tearful baby? Soothe her.

When we dare to give words to our nurture and when we voice them in playgrounds with new friends, we are answering the battle cry.

Because we are many, we are many, we are many.

■　■　■

You unlock your phone during another night feed. You've read that the blue light of the screen isn't great for baby's sleep, or yours, but this is your third wake-up of the night, and you've made peace with trading sleep hygiene for a little scrolling.

You move between apps and swipe past pictures and videos of perfectly sleeping babies from friends and strangers alike.

"Sleeping through at six weeks!" one post reads, and the comments are a mix of *congratulations* and *tellmehow*.

You glance down at your own baby, fast asleep, yet simultaneously still feeding a little. You attempt to unlatch her, but she flinches and begins feeding again with gusto.

"No more night feeds for us!" Another post glows from your screen.

You shuffle a little, getting comfy in your familiar rocker, and begin the nightly ritual of back-and-forth until your baby girl settles back to sleep.

"Why You Shouldn't Rock Your Baby to Sleep: And What to Do Instead!" Your screen is tormenting you, you're certain, so you click the "off" button on your phone, allowing the darkness to consume the room again.

And oddly enough, or perhaps not, the darkness brings nothing but quiet relief.

■ ■ ■

For us to see something as normal, we have to actually *see* it. And the more we see something, the more normalized it becomes. This is how the idea of "normal" is built and cemented, and the reason why social norms can differ so vastly to biological norms.

The media plays a role, including social media, in defining and curating our norms, of course. And even as savvy consumers, it's still so easy to fall into the trap of comparison, especially when we're navigating vulnerable stages of life. Because in times of change or vulnerability, such as the postpartum period and early parenthood in general, we often look outside of ourselves for steadying; we cross compare and use social norms as a barometer of kinds, to answer the deep-set questions that we're toying with: Are we on the right track? Are we doing it right? Are we surrounded by others doing it how we're doing it, or are we, in fact, all alone?

Our cultural values shape our parenting, and in turn, this impacts our children's daily rhythms and behaviors, including sleep. We inevitably witness a push toward independent sleeping arrangements and behavioral-based sleep interventions, such as sleep training, in cultures that place a greater value on independence from a young age.[94] Conversely, we see practices such as bed-sharing and breastfeeding to term in more "nurture-centric" cultures, which are more culturally prone to accept dependency as a given during infancy and the early years of childhood.[95]

While our babies' sleep remains biologically driven,[96] we cannot easily untangle ourselves from the cultural narratives and pressures that we find ourselves parenting within. And so, though unaltered at its core, sleep *can* still be impacted by the cultural values of caregivers and the boarder community at large. Be it through specific sleeping arrangements, levels of responsivity, or even the day-to-day rhythms and routines that we take for granted as being normal, each of these culturally rooted practices can impact or *shape* our babies' sleep.

Such culturally specific values are often woven and entrenched deep within the fabric of society and family structures. We see them, clear as day, on our phone screens, and we hear them, loud and insistent, from the conversations and throwaway remarks that are passed down and between family members.

"It wasn't like this in my day!"

"Mine slept like angels!"

"You were sleep trained and turned out fine!"

The family system that we're born into and raised within can be especially powerful in shaping our own perceptions of what normal looks like in all areas, including infant sleep. If we were independent sleepers from an early age, comments and questions from family members about our babies' contact naps or co-sleeping can be common.

"We're happy doing it our way," the words are delivered with a smile, but there's a hint of something else buried deep.

Frustration? No.

Loneliness? More likely.

Because it can feel isolating to change a family narrative. To choose a different path. To break a cycle.

In the 1970s, the concept of "Ghosts in the Nursery"[97] was introduced by a research team interested in the influence of past generational trauma on current parenting practices and the developing child. The team likened unresolved issues to "ghosts" that haunt present interactions between parents and their children, often leading to the repetition and intergenerational transmission of dysfunctional patterns. With infant sleep, these "ghosts" are more likely to show up when following a generic plan or "fitting in" with expectations instead of following the cues of the unique baby in front of us (even when it means we do things differently to our closest kin).

In contrast, the concept of "Angels in the Nursery"[98] was introduced by another research team in 2005. This time, the "angels" symbolize positive parenting practices and interactions that are passed down from one generation to the next. We can think of "angels" in this context as positive legacies. They are our best memories of our own childhood, repeated or reflected with our babies.

"I remember falling asleep in the car and my dad carrying me to bed when we got home. I always pretended to be fast asleep the whole way to bed, even though I'd woken up, just because I loved how he tucked me in."

"I remember my mom singing to me every night as I fell asleep. She always said she couldn't sing, but her voice was perfect to me."

"I loved Sunday mornings the best. We would all jump inside Mom and Dad's bed before making pancakes together. Pancakes are still my favorite food, even today, all because of those Sunday mornings."

These positive legacies hold a deep-set power, with memories like this serving as a template for sensitive, responsive, and nurturing parenting practices with our own children. It's so much easier to lean into nurture at sleep times if we have even one positive recollection of being nurtured at sleep times during our own early years. And if not, your nurture is powerful enough to create "angels" for your own babies so that in the future, they can rest within the foundations you set yourself. Foundations that are carved by trusting your instincts and the evidence, both the heart and the science, as opposed to hand-me-down snippets of advice that don't serve you or your babies best.

And if you do find yourself carving a brand-new path for you and your children, please know that there are many, many others out there softly carving, too. You're not the only one doing it this way.

■ ■ ■

"You slept in my bed every night for years!"

You turn to face your own mother, puzzled.

"I did?"

"Oh yes! I couldn't get you out of there! You were my sidekick night and day," your mom smiles, "and I didn't mind it one bit."

She offers your daughter a raspberry and puts another into her own mouth. The pair look like long lost friends, one big, one small, sharing berry secrets together in your kitchen on a rainy weekday lunchtime.

"Not that I could ever tell anyone about it," your mom sighs, "there wasn't much support back then, you know?"

"I don't remember that at all," you shake your head and wipe raspberry juice from the table.

"I think you do," your mom is talking to you, but gazing at your daughter, "somewhere inside, you remember."

"More!" Your daughter reaches up and stretches out her hand for another raspberry, and without pause, your mom leans across the table and places one gently into her palm.

■ ■ ■

Pause

"My friends' babies sleep through in their cribs, but mine still wakes and co-sleeps."

Your baby's answer: "I'm awake again, mama. I know you've read that I should be sleeping through the night by now, and I'm sure there are other babies who do that every night. In time, I'll do that too, mama, I really will. But for now, I need these middle-of-the-night check-ins with you. I need my milk, and I need your arms. I love it most when we sleep close together, but I won't always need you right here. Soon, too soon really, I'll sleep in my own bed, and you can stretch out in yours. There might even be moments where you'll miss these nighttime check-ins together. I know they're hard right now, though, and that you miss sleeping longer stretches. I just hope you know that what you're doing is important. You're helping me sleep better, not worse, both right now and for the future too. Thank you for being here with me, mama, awake again, but together."

Prompt: Do you tend to compare your baby's sleep to others?

Rest Assured, a Nurturing Approach

If you feel alone in your nighttime nurturing, it can help to connect with others who are also opting to meet nighttime needs with connection and nurture, since maternal support systems can play a critical role in buffering stress in the early years.[99] Being able to openly talk about how your baby is sleeping (or not), without fear of judgment, can help normalize the idea and practice of nighttime nurturing, making it feel less lonely and more manageable overall.

The Power of Reflection

As a practical exercise, parental reflection can bring clarity in this season. Looking back on our own childhood sleep experiences can help us reframe expectations, gain insight into our responses, and build confidence in our choices as we support our children's sleep.

Why does this matter?

Because when parents feel grounded, supported, and emotionally regulated, babies feel safer and more secure, both of which support sleep.

Research shows that heightened parental emotional availability, responsivity, and attunement are all connected with a direct improvement in nighttime sleep for babies,[100,101,102] and a supported, steady, and settled parent is a parent who is well equipped to deliver such availability, responsivity, and attunement.

Yet, feeling steady as a parent doesn't always happen automatically; it is something we cultivate over time. Reflection gives us a moment to pause, process, and make sense of our own feelings, which in turn:

- Reduces self-doubt by allowing us to recognize why certain sleep practices feel intuitive (or why they feel difficult)
- Strengthens our sense of purpose by helping us see the bigger picture beyond the tiredness of the moment
- Fosters self-compassion by highlighting the love and care we pour into our babies, even if sleep feels unpredictable

You and your baby are an interconnected team, after all. Taking a moment to reflect on your own memories of sleep during childhood can be a powerful way to gain insight and perspective:

Did sleep feel safe and inviting?
Were your cries and calls answered?
Did you experience nighttime anxiety or fears?

It can be both difficult and healing to give freely what was never received, and this is where parental reflection or "reparenting" supports us to break cycles and allows for the creation of "angels," or positive patterns of behavior in relation to sleep.

In practical terms, this might look like rocking your baby to sleep without worrying about bad habits, responding to cries while trusting that comfort fosters long-term security, and trusting cues over generic sleep plans, with the firm recognition that no two babies are the same.

(continued)

These small, conscious choices, made mindfully, intentionally, and without fear, not only meet the needs of the child in
your arms, but also honor the child you once were. And sometimes, honoring that child means standing firm in the quiet,
even when it feels like you're the only one doing it this way.

Just for a Moment, Let's Pretend. . .

Whether or not your childhood sleep memories are positive,
and whether or not you have a close-knit network to hold
and support you now, I can assure you that there are many,
many others raising babies with nurture, heart, and science,
just like you.

But just for a moment, let's pretend that there aren't.

Just for second or two, let's pretend you really are the only one:

The only one with a wakeful baby.
The only one responding to cries with care.
*The only one holding your baby in your arms and rock-
ing or feeding as they drift off to sleep.*

Would it change a thing?

Zoom in, close, and ask yourself:

*If I really was the only one doing it this way, would it
be so bad?*
Would I stop responding?
Would I stop soothing?

Or would you continue to carve the path that works for you
and the unique child in your arms?

Because you're not the only one. Not by a long way.

But if you were?

I suspect you'd nurture on, regardless.

CHAPTER 11

Sleep Will Come

It's 8 p.m. and your newborn is crying.

"I don't know what he needs," your voice cracks.

"Can you feed him?" Your husband's suggestion feels like a mountain to climb.

"I just fed him. . . ."

"Maybe feed him again?"

You pick up your baby boy and try to latch him to your breast. You wince as his jaw clamps down. His tears have stopped, but yours flow alongside your milk.

Your baby settles toward sleep but remains latched. Your own tiredness rises, alongside the doubts.

Is this how it will be now? Perma-latched and perma-awake, with a child who will only sleep in arms?

Just days into this new role of mother and already you feel lost. Like you have no idea what to do. Like you don't know the way forward from here.

"He's falling asleep," your husband whispers, softly.

"You're doing it," his voice is your anchor.

"Keep going, sleep will come."

■ ■ ■

When we're surrounded by diapers and burp cloths and figuring each day out as we go, it can feel really, really hard to see beyond the current stage and to trust that sleep will one day feel less all-consuming. Because that's how it tends to feel in the early days; our lack of autonomy at night and the insistence of our babies on our caregiving inevitably becomes a focal point.

Louise, help! My baby is four weeks old, and he doesn't know the difference between night and day! He sleeps all afternoon and is wide awake when the sun sets!

Louise, I'm writing this after being awake for the last hour, nursing. It's 1:30 a.m. right now, and I can't help but feel like I'm doing something wrong. He's six weeks old. What can I do to help him sleep?

Louise, is there a sleep regression at eight weeks? I was told they should be sleeping by themselves by now, but my little one will ONLY sleep when I'm holding him!

These are the notes that land in my inbox each day. They land as unfiltered glimpses into the realities of days and nights spent doubting:

> Am I doing it right?
> Will it always be this hard?
> Will I ever sleep again?

At the highest level my reply is yes, no, and yes, in exactly that order. Yet when we dig deeper, we can see interconnected roots that merge and work together to support these answers.

Because a newborn without a clear day-to-night distinction is a normal newborn. An infant who feeds during the night is a normal infant. A baby who rests best in arms is a normal baby.

As humans, we map our wakeful hours to the sun, and this mapping happens at a chemical level, whereby sensors in our eyes let our brains know to release certain hormones, depending on the level of light exposure taking place.

Yet, the circadian system is not fully developed at birth, even though entrainment to day and night begins during pregnancy, as a passive response to maternal melatonin secretion. This is why newborn babies typically exhibit a polyphasic sleep pattern, sleeping in several short bursts throughout any given 24-hour period, without a distinction between day and night. And yet, with the natural passage of time, comes development. This development may not be super obvious or even discussed, but during the first three months post-birth, we see the emergence and entrainment of melatonin and cortisol secretion to a circadian rhythm.[103]

Our babies' sleep is developing, just as it should.

By four months of age, most infants have developed a more defined circadian rhythm, whereby baby's body starts to synchronize more effectively with natural environmental cues, and by six months, circadian rhythms are seen to be fully expressed.

"Environmental cues?" My friend is side-eyeing me again.

"He lives in the world, isn't that enough? It goes dark at night, so shouldn't he sleep?"

When we look at the biology of human sleep, environmental cues are an essential factor in how and when we fall asleep and how long we sleep for. They're a big deal. While we cannot force this entrainment or natural development of the circadian system, we can absolutely support it by working with and facilitating healthy and appropriate cues, and perhaps the most significant environmental cue is *light exposure.*

Specifically, sensitivity of the circadian pacemaker is heightened in the morning and evening. Exposure to bright evening light is related to a *phase delay* of sleep, whereby babies grow sleepy later (and wake up later), while exposure to bright morning light is related to a *phase advance* of sleep, whereby little ones feel sleepy earlier in the evening (and wake earlier in the morning). Bright light during the middle of the day, meanwhile, has less of a direct influence on the pacemaker but still supports sleep at bedtime. The good news is that we can use this knowledge to help support a robust circadian system for our babies, via *safe* exposure to natural light, each and every day.

This might look like spending a few minutes outside within an hour of waking each morning. Or, it might consist of getting outside during the middle of the day, being sure not to exceed a safe level of sun exposure. Working with these environmental cues might also include the avoidance of artificial, blue-spectrum lights in the evening. We can also optimize daylight exposure during daytime naps by avoiding total darkness at nap times. We, as humans, are so primed for this day-to-night synchronization that even with closed eyelids, our bodies are still able to receive these external cues via light exposure.

Food also acts as an environmental cue to support baby's circadian rhythm. Breastfed babies benefit form indirect entrainment through exposure to maternal melatonin levels via breast milk, for instance. For moms who pump, it's recommended to note the time-of-day milk is pumped so that baby can be fed daytime milk during the daytime and nighttime milk during night feeds. For older babies and toddlers, offering meals and snacks at relatively consistent times can help to establish predictable metabolic cycles. This is because food intake is a powerful time cue for the body's peripheral circadian clocks, and the circadian system is best supported when there is alignment between the peripheral and central clocks.

"So, milk on tap, naps without block-out blinds, no screens before bed, and he'll be sleeping through?" my friend is only half-joking.

"Well, if the shoe fits. . .," I offer, only half-joking, too.

■ ■ ■

It's 9 p.m. and your baby is wide awake after just 40 minutes of sleep.

You're six months into motherhood and six months into questioning whether you'll ever feel rested again.

"Back in the rocking chair," you text your friend, "this is my life now LOL."

But you aren't laughing.

"He's at that age," your friend replies straightaway, most likely from her own rocking chair, too.

"You're doing it," your phone pings again.

"Keep going, sleep will come."

■ ■ ■

The first year can feel like a mosaic of firsts and lasts and leaps, all thrown together in the depths of long, wakeful nights where we inevitably begin to question whether our babies will ever, ever, sleep through.

They will, though I know that can be hard to believe when we're "in it."

"Louise, we do bath, book then bed. It's a solid routine, and he still will not sleep without a fuss!"

"Louise, I have his sleep space set up so nicely; it's dark enough and not too cold or too hot, but he's waking more than ever."

"Louise, I don't know what I'm doing differently because out of nowhere, he isn't sleeping! I've changed nothing about his bedtime or nights at all. What am I missing?"

When we're doing everything that we've been told we must do, and still, our babies are not sleeping in the way that we've been told they should be sleeping, it is so easy to question:

What am I missing?

The answer to this question that keeps cropping up, especially in the depths of the night, is that you're not missing anything; it's all right here, but much like a mosaic, the pieces of the sleep puzzle are segmented.

And so, if you find yourself questioning, it can help to take a broader view of the full "puzzle" of sleep, focusing especially on how and why humans grow tired.

Paired with the circadian driver of human sleep is our homeostatic sleep drive. This is also known as sleep pressure or, more simply, tiredness. With prolonged periods of waking, we naturally grow tired enough to sleep. The higher sleep pressure builds, the sleepier we feel, and when we fall asleep, the accumulated pressure is relieved, so our tiredness levels fall again.

If you're doing everything "by the book" and your thriving baby is especially wakeful, supporting the homeostatic sleep drive can bring so much sleep relief, and quickly. The idea here is to optimize tiredness. It's the Goldilocks effect for sleep: not too much, and not too little. Just right is the aim, but of course, this varies from child to child.

Some babies, with higher sleep needs, will tire very easily, their sleep pressure accumulating quickly. Other babies, with lower sleep needs, will require more input and stimulation to grow tired, their sleep pressure accumulating slowly. Working with the baby and individualized sleep needs in front of us is key when optimizing this sleep drive.

"Oh, he'll sleep tonight!" There's a grandma at the playground with kind and knowing eyes.

She nods her head toward a toddler who is climbing up the slide for the fourth time before whooshing back down again.

"I sure hope so," the little boy's mom calls back with a smile, visibly relieved that the slide climbing isn't mentioned.

"Mark my words, he'll wear himself out with all that climbing!"

The idea of letting our babies and toddlers wear themselves out was once a pretty standard expectation. It was widely accepted that the more children move, explore, and play, the more tired they would be by bedtime, and this was seen as the goal. Tire them. Exhaust them even. Wear them out.

Now, though, we are collectively terrified of launching our little ones into the realm of overtiredness. And because of this, we are collectively minimizing energy expenditure and protecting rest times with every ounce of energy that we have left. The idea of a skipped nap looms heavy. A late night is not an option. A tired baby is a fail.

But what if it isn't?

We know, now, that everyday tiredness (and even overtiredness) is not pathogenic. It's the result of a busy day spent learning and moving and existing in the world. And when we look more closely at how homeostatic sleep pressure forms, it is the simplest, most everyday moments of the human experience that build healthy sleep pressure. This is good news, because it makes supporting this sleep drive even more accessible and, dare I say it, easy.

Because we all tend to sleep better after a day spent moving our bodies and working our muscles. Motor skill practice, at any age and stage, is extremely helpful for supporting and building sleep pressure. For babies and young children, rolling, crawling, walking, pushing, pulling, running, and jumping are all age-specific key ingredients for a good night's sleep. The key, no matter which stage of development your little one is currently navigating, is to facilitate time and space for movement. A child on the cusp of crawling, for instance, will have a body and brain that's wired for and driven toward practicing that new skill repeatedly until it is integrated and acquired. Free time spent on the floor doesn't only support skill development; it supports sleep, too.

"You've got your hands full with that one!"

The slide-climbing toddler has more than accomplished crawling, and the playground grandma chuckles, though her words sound more like a remembering.

The little boy is now pushing his hands into the muddy patch at the bottom of the slide. He squelches the earth between his fingers, before wiping streaks across the pale blue of his jacket.

"He's learning," the grandma smiles, "and nature sure is a good teacher!"

Muddy hands are a staple of these early years. We might balk at the mess or roll our eyes at the ever-growing pile of laundry, but there is a name for what nature is offering our babies: sensory nourishment. That is, the natural stimulation of baby's senses. Sensory nourishment is often overlooked in our culture of busy schedules, but it's a key element of supporting the homeostatic sleep drive, because our babies are wired to expect and experience a complex sensory environment. With rich sensory stimulation, infant brains and bodies are free to function within and process their external environment in a healthy and age-appropriate way. This is at the heart of why babies often fall asleep more easily after spending just a short period of time outside in the fresh air. The more we can facilitate and allow for the natural stimulation of baby's senses, the more "ready" for sleep our little ones will be by bedtime, due to the dream-team of heightened sleep pressure and a regulated nervous system.

Such sensory nourishment may be as simple as an hour spent outside, touching the earth without gloves or shoes, feeling the softness of a flower petal, or even listening to birdsong. This nourishment lies in the moments within moments we, as adults, are so primed to ignore. Yet, our little ones are still unmolded by society's expectations and so they come into this world ready to pause and notice: the sound of the birds first thing in the morning, the way the light flickers through the trees, the sheer satisfaction of squeezing fresh mud through tiny fingers.

When they climb the slide.

When they press their hands into mud.

When they stop to examine yet-another-rock on the path.

Our little ones are learning, and sleep pressure is building, bit by bit, muddy handprint by muddy handprint.

■ ■ ■

It's 10 p.m. on the evening of your baby's first birthday, and he's woken for a feed.

Your mind swirls after a busy afternoon spent celebrating your little one's big day, and the quiet of the nursery feels blissful after so much chatter and excitement.

Moments from the last year run through your head. It's been a year of firsts. A year of memories. A year of highs and lows. And the baby in your arms is so much bigger now, but still so new.

Other people's words from earlier in the day swirl, too, in the periphery:

> "Wait, he's still waking?"
> "Have you not fixed his sleep yet?"
> "It's because you haven't weaned him yet!"

But your baby interrupts your thoughts, his eyes opening momentarily, mid-feed.

He smiles up at you, sleepily, and your mind quietens, instantly.

"You're doing it," he seems to be willing.

"Keep going, sleep will come."

■ ■ ■

Another boost for our sleep pressure, as humans, is social stimulation. Yet not all social stimulation is created equal. When we're surrounded by people, new faces, or new voices, our brains are working hard to process these connections. This is tiring, intrinsically human work. Yet, it's easy to become overwhelmed, to feel disoriented, or even to dissociate in an effort to maintain a sense of equilibrium when social stimulation becomes *too much* to manage in a healthy way.

It's the Goldilocks effect again; we want to socialize enough, but not too much and ideally with people who feel "just right." Plus, we want to do this on our own terms, which may change from day to day, depending on how we're feeling. Our babies are no different. Some will naturally prefer more social stimulation than others. And there will, inevitably, be variations depending on the day of the week, the time of the day, and the alignment of the moon and stars.

When we find the sweet spot, though, we can fill our little ones' socializing cups just enough to build a healthy level of tiredness, without becoming dysregulated from *too much*.

"Pass him here!" Arms outstretch toward baby, and little hands clasp around strands of mom's hair.

"Does he want his new truck?" A well-meaning offer, accompanied by an all-singing, occasionally flashing, brand new toy truck to play with.

"Um, no thanks, he's getting tired." A polite smile and a quick scan for an exit, while baby's clasped fist tightens a little more.

When we think about boosting sleep drives with social stimulation, it's helpful to avoid the "wired but tired" state that goes hand in hand with certain social environments. These are the places and gatherings we leave feeling more dysregulated than we felt when we arrived. Instead, we want to encourage natural, cup-filling social stimulation whereby baby's sense of safety doesn't falter, even while they are interacting. In practice, this typically involves a trusted caregiver acting as a *bridge* between baby and others.

We are the bridge when we hold baby while everyone settles in.

(We are not "hogging" our own child.)

We are the bridge when we avoid playing "pass-the-baby" during family get-togethers.

(We are not being difficult.)

We are the bridge when we allow and facilitate time and space for our little ones to "warm up" to their new surroundings.

(We are not being antisocial.)

Our goal is to enable healthy socializing and, by default, increase sleep pressure, while supporting baby's felt sense of safety. We are aiming for a regulated child, even within busy and stimulating environments, and this is most likely to occur with us acting as a supportive bridge between baby and the wider world. It's regulation, after all, that promotes healthy and easeful sleep and which allows for that Goldilocks level of "just rightness."

■ ■ ■

It's 11 p.m. and you're heading to bed.

The house is quiet and still, and just as you do every night before bed, you stop outside your son's room and open the door a crack.

The room is dark, and the old rocker sits to one side of his bed, piled high with teddies and soft, well-loved animals.

You venture in to pick up a couple of toys from the floor, without worrying about waking your sleepyhead; if he stirs, you know he'll be back to sleep in seconds.

You kiss his head, as you always have, and he turns over in his sleep.

He's still your baby, though he's bigger now. His arms and legs are long and strong. There's even a scuff on his perfect knee. Just for a second, though, your mind takes you back to his babyhood. There's something about the way he sleeps, the curve of his nose, the sweep of his cheeks, that remain baby soft.

You're doing it.

A mantra from years earlier creeps into your mind.

Keep going, sleep will come.

These are the words that carried you through, but right now, you allow time to stand still, just for a moment.

It feels like yesterday that your sweet baby fit entirely in your arms.

You kiss his head again, and his eyes flicker open.

"Mama's here," you whisper, as you always have, "Love you."

"Love you too," he whispers back, before rolling over again and falling right back to sleep.

■ ■ ■

Pause

"My baby still wakes at night."

Your baby's answer: "I know I look bigger, mama, but I still need you at night. I promise I won't wake and call for you like this forever. One day, I'll drift off to sleep all by myself, and you'll wonder how I grew so quickly. Soon enough, our nights will stretch out, and we won't see each other until morning. How strange, mama, to think of that now, when your arms and voice meet me in the darkness night after night. One day, I'll surprise you with just how long I can sleep, and we will look back at these moments spent together in the quiet with peace, not regret. Thank you for trusting my timeline, mama. I know you're tired, but you're doing it. Keep going, sleep will come."

Prompt: Take a moment to imagine yourself, several years from now, remembering this season of wakeful nights. Which moments might you hold onto, with a sense of peace and just-rightness?

Rest Assured, a Nurturing Approach

For this pause, I wanted to offer both affirmations and practical, step-by-step resources.

If you're in the season of frequent wakes, navigating changing routines, or simply wanting gentle guidance that honors your instincts, there's nurture-rooted support available. Scan the following QR code to access a library of support and resources to support you.

With support, sleep can be stress-free and truly restful.

Rest Assured, Affirmations to Support Your Journey
- ◆ I am my baby's safe haven.
- ◆ I am my baby's secure base.
- ◆ This is important work.
- ◆ My baby's brain grows best through love.
- ◆ I accept peaceful rest in all its forms.
- ◆ I understand and support my child's needs.
- ◆ I understand and support my own needs.
- ◆ My child and I are a perfect team.
- ◆ Keep going, sleep will come.

CHAPTER 12

You Are the Great, Great, Great Granddaughter This World Needs

You are four years old.

Your baby brother is tired and cranky, and your mom is dancing with him, from side to side.

"Mama's here," she whispers softly, and the words you've heard a thousand times wrap around your brother.

You watch the way your mom sways, her arms wrapped around her newest baby's body and her cheek pressed against his head as she whispers.

"Mama's here," her words are balm and your brother's cries quieten, but the swaying continues.

You choose a crayon carefully from the tub on the table and draw three circles in a row on your notepad. One big, two small. You dot and swipe eyes, noses, and mouths in almost all the right places, and draw a red heart around it all.

"It's us," you whisper, too, handing the drawing to Mom.

Her eyes are heavy with tiredness, but she smiles nonetheless.

"Oh wow, it's us?" she asks, delighted.

You nod.

"All wrapped up in a heart?" she asks, pausing to give the drawing her precious attention.

You might well be glowing with pride, as you nod again.

"It's a love bubble," you offer.

Tears fill your mom's eyes, but you do not worry. You know these tears. They are her love tears. They are perfect, just like Mom.

"I'll put this by my bed so I can look at it every night at bedtime," a perfect promise, as she sits down on the sofa, your brother now sleeping across her chest.

You pull a book from the shelf and plod across to the sofa, too, while your mom makes a safe space for you to squeeze in close.

"Three in a row, just like your picture" she smiles, and she wraps an arm around you to begin your story.

■ ■ ■

I don't know my great, great, great grandmother's name, though sometimes, I wonder what it would be like to travel back in time, just for a moment, to meet her.

Would she recognize me?

A distant granddaughter, separated by births and years; would she recognize the way I hold my babies, the nighttime whispers I offer them, the tiredness I've carried?

I think of researchers, quantifying development on charts and within papers, and I feel grateful yet bemused: grateful that we have the proof now to support our instincts and bemused that we need it to fight against the overriding tide. Because we now know, categorically, that children thrive through nurture. We know that closeness grows brains. We know that infants sleep entirely differently than adults. And yet we are still surrounded by a ripple effect of low-nurture caregiving. Our society, as a whole, is a low-nurture society. In too many instances, we are more like to be ridiculed or shamed for responding to the nighttime calls of our babies, than supported.

And therein lies the work.

The work to change the narrative and disrupt the ripple of trauma and dysfunction that's quietly making its way from one generation to the next, unless and until there comes a soul who is brave enough to challenge and change course. It is just one generation of cycle breakers who could change the world for the better, after all.

Whether or not you are the great, great, great granddaughter of a swaying, responsive, night-nurturing parent or not, every time you find yourself swaying in the darkness with your own baby, responding with tenderness to cries, and soothing through the night, you are realigning the status quo, just a little, back toward nurture.

You're doing the work, and make no mistake, you're doing it beautifully.

■ ■ ■

You are dancing with your baby, by the light of the moon.

Well, technically, you are swaying from side to side, baby in arms, as you gaze out of the nursery window at 2 a.m.

You are tired and your bones feel heavy from the lack of sleep, and yet, you simultaneously feel brand new. Your body, your mind, your schedule; everything has altered and adjusted to this new being you're holding close.

Your daughter squirms a little and you swap the swaying for stillness, just for a moment.

You catch your reflection in the window, draped in your comfiest cardigan, arms full of baby, belly still round and soft, hair half up, half down, and knotted.

This is it, you realize.

This, right here, in the depths of the night, is what it's all about.

Because you are undone. There is nowhere to hide at 2 a.m. There is only you and your baby and the transient windows of sleep that you both move between.

You trace a finger over your daughter's brow, down her cheek and across her chin. She is perfection. She does not fidget or falter. She breathes deep, instead.

The sigh of safety.

All these years of smiling in all the right places and doing as you were told in just the way you were expected to do it. All these years of climbing career ladders and navigating friendship circles and striving to prove yourself. And here you are, brand new, hair askew and cardigan draped, safekeeper of the most precious soul.

This is important, you realize.

This matters, you're sure.

■ ■ ■

When I work with families, no matter the sleep query or circumstance, there is one key concept that I return to time and again: safekeeping.

Not just the practicalities of safe sleep, but also the biology of infant safekeeping, too.

Because when our babies are waking during the night, they are essentially doing so to check for safety. Internally, they are checking their biological status, just as we do as adults. If breathing patterns are compromised, rousing keeps baby safe. If temperature is too high or too low, rousing keeps baby safe. If hunger is increasing, rousing (to feed) keeps baby safe. The check occurs, followed by a cue or communication of the need. This triggers a sensitive and appropriate response in an attentive, high-nurture caregiver, which meets the need, and the need fizzles away, followed by a return to sleep.

Externally, our babies don't yet have the neural architecture to logically scan their environment for predators, intruders, or damage to shelter or terrain. They are not checking whether to go and stoke a fire themselves, as we are wired to do as adults. Instead, they are checking for one thing and one thing only: *is my big person close by?*

Because by default, we are our babies' safety nets. We share our nervous systems, our brains, our arms, and our hearts to ensure that the external environment is safe for our babies to thrive within. Our little ones do not need to understand distance or the logical, culturally specific dangers that may present during the darkness. They simply need our presence, to tick their external safety check box, and to settle down to sleep.

Closeness is a superpower, not a bad habit. It creates and strengthens those feelings of safety that wire a baby's brain to expect safety in and from the world. These are the brains wired for trust, compassion, and relationship. They are the brains wired for connection first. They are the brains wired for healthy, stress-free, *rest.*

■   ■   ■

You are lying in your bed, awake.

Your eyes are wide open, and your ears strained, listening for the familiar *click* of the door.

"Call me if you need me," you type the words into your phone and press Send.

An eternity passes within a couple of minutes.

"Home soon, don't worry!"

You breathe out, and your mind reaches back, all the way back, to a time when the calls came relentlessly, each and every night.

At some point, the cries turned into, "Mama," which turned into, "Mommy," which turned into, "Mom," and all along, these calls grew less insistent and far, far less frequent.

"Call me if you need me," you would whisper as you kissed her still-rounded cheek. And sure enough, she would, and you'd leave your bed and make your way to hers in the dark glow of the night. You'd squeeze in beside her and she'd rest the back of her hand against your neck, as always. It felt like an eternity, and also just a blink.

"You're safe and loved," you would whisper into the stillness of the room, even after sleep had arrived.

The sound of a car's engine pulls you from your thoughts and you listen carefully.

Click.

Safe, you breathe in.

And loved, you breathe out.

Always.

■ ■ ■

I am writing these words after a good night's sleep. I am through the fog of the earliest days of raising babies, and I can tell you that I do not regret one single second of supporting my children's sleep.

They sleep beautifully, by the way.

Though we've never aimed for 7 p.m. until 7 a.m., without rousing.

My youngest loves his sleep. He falls asleep peacefully and sleeps all the way through until his sleep needs are met in the morning. Some nights that looks like 8 p.m. until 8 a.m., and others it looks more like 8:30 p.m. until 7 a.m. Occasionally, he'll wake with the birds in the early hours, but he will roll over and fall back to sleep if he's still feeling tired. There's such ease in the way that he sleeps.

My eldest falls asleep quickly after a busy day, though some nights she will wake for a drink or to pull up her covers to get a little more cozy. She's always been a sensitive sleeper, and when she was tiny, she would turn to me for soothing. Now though, she doesn't need me to help reach her drink or tuck her in. She breezes through night times with security and independence. She soothes herself.

There are a couple of nights each year when we can see fireworks from our kitchen window. During our most recent kitchen display, I was standing by the window, watching the colors as they danced across the sky, when I heard footsteps.

"Hi," my daughter whispered.

She wandered over to me and rested her head on my shoulder (because that is how tall she is now), and there we stood, quietly watching the sky together, in the darkness of the kitchen. I did not worry about her getting back to sleep. I did not have to rock her or pace the floor. When the fireworks stopped, she kissed my cheek goodnight and made her way back to her own bed, in her own room, where she slept the rest of the night through.

Meanwhile, my husband and son were both fast asleep, each completely undisturbed and unbothered by the bangs and crackles lighting up the sky.

Before climbing into bed beside my husband, I stopped off at our son's room. I wondered in (I don't need to tiptoe) and I adjusted his covers. Not because he needed it, simply because I wanted to. I pushed a stray curl from his face and kissed his forehead, just as I do every night.

"You are safe and loved," I told him, as always, and he sighed his sigh of safety.

Asleep, but aware. Aware of being cared for, of being kept safe, of being loved.

What a gift.

■　■　■

You are a grandmother.

Your babies have grown and have babies of their own, and you are living the early years all over again, albeit from the periphery.

This time, you are not the one who's awake and soothing at 2 a.m. You are not the one who's sharing your body, your arms and your identity with the brand new being who looks so much like your own baby girl did years ago, or was it just yesterday? The years feel like both a lifetime and a moment, simultaneously. They stretch into the past, sometimes merged and blended, and other times clear as day.

You sit, granddaughter in arms, gazing into the most familiar of eyes. You see your mother, yourself, your daughter, and now your granddaughter within them. It catches your breath to see time mapped out like this: so transient, fleeting, and yet so insistent.

Your early years of motherhood felt like a marathon. A quest of figuring it out. Of avoiding mistakes. Of trying, endlessly trying, to do the right thing. You remember the loneliness of nighttime wake-ups. You remember the guilt of offering closeness, connection, and soothing when everyone else had been so certain that only disconnect would do. You remember the warnings, loud and clear.

"You'll be sorry," they were certain.

"You're making your life harder," they were unwavering.

"You'll live to regret it," they were sure.

And yet, at one or several points along the way, the quest became more of a meandering. A slower, calmer journey along a path that felt safe.

Thank goodness.

You sit with your granddaughter in your arms while your daughter sips a warm drink beside you. She leans into you and gently, oh so beautifully, maps the curve of her baby's button nose with her fingertip.

"We spent the whole morning contact napping," she whispers, calm and sure in her nurture. She sets her cup down and rests her head against your shoulder, in just the same way she did as a child. Then, she sighs.

The sigh of safety.

Your breath catches again and never before has it been clearer; you aren't sorry for a single second spent pacing the nursery floor. You did not make your life harder by bringing your children into the big bed in the early morning hours. And you do not regret a single moment spent nurturing your babies.

■ ■ ■

We've been here a while, mama, rocking back and forth, and I know you must miss your bed.

Your eyes keep closing, just like mine, but you still hum in the darkness. I love your hums, mama.

I've fallen asleep a few times at least, but tonight is one of those nights where I wake just as often as I sleep.

I know these nights are hard, mama, and I hope you know how much I love that you're here with me.

Soon, we won't have so many of these nights. Soon, we'll look back on nights like this and wonder how we ever managed to find such peace among the waking.

Because that's what you bring me, mama: peace. It's in your arms, and the way that you rock me, and the hums that you hum in just the perfect way that you hum them.

One day, I'll have the words to thank you for the rocking and the humming and the peace, mama. If I could, I'd I'll tell you today that this work that you're doing in the depths of the night is important, and you're doing it beautifully. If I could, I'd let you know that you, just as you are, are everything I need. One day, too soon really, I'll have the words, mama, but for now, I hope you can feel my silent thank you in the way that I calm almost instantly when you hold me close, and sleep so easily when I'm in your arms.

"Mama's here," your perfect hums turn to perfect whispers.

"Thank you, Mama," I want to whisper back, "Thank you."

Epilogue

*H**ow to write a book?*
Write what you know to be true.

These pages are what I know to be true. They carry the words that I wish every parent navigating these intense, wonderful, and exhausting early years could read. They hold both the heart and the science of nurturing baby sleep in such a way that's designed to bring more ease, and peace, to this season of life.

Because when everyone around us is telling us to cry it out, we need to know that sleep training hasn't always been the go-to. We need to know that human babies have thrived (and slept) without training for thousands upon thousands of years. We need to know that our great, great, great grandmothers didn't sleep train their babies.

And when it feels hard, so hard, to function on little sleep, with a baby near-constantly on the hip and living in a world that expects us to *bounce back* in every single way after birth, we need to know that it feels hard because it is hard.

And when our children insist on closeness, even though the rest of the world expects their independence, we need to know that it isn't our babies who are misguided.

And when we feed and feed and feed some more throughout the night in the early months, we need to know that we aren't causing our little ones' night waking by offering milk, by holding them close, or by soothing them. We are supporting their sleep every time we answer their calls.

And when the world seems sure, so sure, that without teaching or training, our babies will simply never learn how to sleep by themselves, we need to know that sleep isn't a skill we are tasked with teaching. It's a biological function that begins before birth and which develops over time. We need to trust that our babies already know how to sleep.

And when our babies settle in our arms and sigh their big sighs before drifting off to sleep, we need to know that offering comfort and soothing is never, ever, a bad habit.

And when our children cling to us, unapologetic in their absolute need for closeness, we need to know that clingy babies are normal babies.

And when we birth a baby who wakes more frequently than our friends' babies do, or who seems to need more comfort, more soothing, and more closeness overall, we need to know that it's okay, wonderful even, that this new being, this brand-new baby, isn't like the others.

And when the days feel long, so long, and the hours drag on, we need the reminder that the intensity will pass. That even the hardest moments are temporary. That everything changes.

And when we feel like the only one, we need to know that there are other mothers in other homes in other towns, cities, and even eras, who are carving similar, nurture-rooted paths.

And when we are tired all the way down to our bones, we need to know that sleep will come.

And when our choices feel like they fall outside of the norm and we're met with raised brows and shakes of the head, we need to remember that these are the choices of a great, great, great granddaughter that this world so desperately needs.

For me, personally, years into this work, if I were to meet my new-mama self again, I would hand her these pages. Then, I would cook her a hot meal, clean up the dishes afterward, and let her rest with her baby.

"This is important work," I'd tell her, "And you're doing it."

"Rest assured," I'd whisper, "You're doing a hard job, and you're doing it beautifully."

About the Author

Louise Herbert is a pediatric sleep and development specialist, accredited in sleep science, perinatal–infant mental health, and infant feeding. She is the founder of Mother Nourish Nurture, a trusted platform supporting families with gentle, evidence-based guidance through the early years.

Louise also leads an internationally recognized certification program for professionals working with babies, toddlers, and families. Her work is redefining how infant sleep is understood, centering biological norms and the transformative power of nurture.

She lives by the ocean in Australia with her husband and two children, and continues to advocate for care that is both grounded in science and attuned to the emotional reality of parenthood.

(Scan the QR code to find out more about Louise.)

Glossary of Terms

Active sleep   A state of sleep characterized by rapid eye movements, irregular breathing, and increased brain activity, similar to REM sleep in adults.

Attachment   A bio-behavioral system, which exists to support infant safety and survival.

Attunement   Awareness, comprehension, and responsivity to an infant's emotional and physiological cues.

Autonomic nervous system (ANS)   The part of the nervous system that controls involuntary bodily functions, including heart rate, digestion, respiration, and sleep–wake cycles.

Behaviorism   A psychological theory that emphasizes environmental conditioning over innate traits.

Biphasic sleep   A sleep pattern consisting of two distinct periods of sleep within a 24-hour cycle.

Chronotype   An individual's natural inclination for sleep and wake times, often categorized as morning types (early birds) or evening types (night owls).

Circadian pacemaker   A group of neurons in the brain's suprachiasmatic nucleus that regulates the body's internal clock and circadian rhythm.

Circadian rhythm   The natural, biological cycle that regulates sleep–wake patterns, hormone release, and other physiological processes over a roughly 24-hour period.

Co-regulation   The interconnected regulation of emotions and physiological states between individuals.

Cuddle curl   A sleeping position in which a caregiver curls around their baby, often promoting safety and responsiveness during co-sleeping.

Dream feed   A late-night feed offered to an infant while they are drowsy.

Exterogestation   A period of time, after birth, where infants continue to develop outside the womb, or "externally gestate."

Homeostatic sleep drive   Also known as sleep pressure, the homeostatic sleep drive refers to the natural, biological need to sleep that builds up during waking hours.

Hypersomnia   Excessive sleepiness or prolonged sleep duration at inappropriate times.

Hyposomnia   Reduced sleep duration or quality, leading to fatigue and impaired functioning.

Hypothalamic–pituitary–adrenal (HPA) axis A complex neuroendocrine system that regulates the stress response and supports homeostasis (internal balance and stability within the body).

Industrial revolution A historical period of rapid, industry-based, economic, and social change.

Insecure attachment A classification of attachment that arises from interactions that fail to meet a child's need for security, understanding, and emotional connection. Insecure attachment can manifest in different patterns, including anxious-resistant, avoidant, and disorganized.

Melatonin A hormone produced by the pineal gland, which helps control the body's sleep–wake cycle.

Moro reflex An involuntary protective motor response that occurs in response to sudden stimulation of an abrupt disruption of balance.

Myelination The process of forming a protective sheath around neurons, to improve the speed and efficiency of nerve signal transmission.

Neural pruning The natural process where unused neural connections are eliminated, to refine brain function and development.

Neurons Cells of the nervous system that transmit information through electrical and chemical signals.

Night terrors Sudden episodes of intense behavior, such as screaming or thrashing, that occur during sleep, and typically without memory of the event.

Non-rapid eye movement (NREM) sleep NREM sleep is divided into stages, each progressively deeper and characterized by distinct brain wave patterns. NREM sleep is crucial for brain development, memory consolidation, physical growth, cellular repair, and immune function.

Object permanence The understanding that objects continue to exist even when they cannot be seen, heard, or touched.

Oxytocin Often referred to as the love hormone, oxytocin is a hormone associated with bonding, relaxation, and social connection.

Parasympathetic nervous system The branch of the autonomic nervous system responsible for relaxation, digestion, and sleep regulation, often referred to as the rest and digest system.

Phase advance of sleep A shift in sleep timing where sleep and wake times occur earlier, often seen in young children and older adults.

Phase delay of sleep A shift in sleep timing where sleep and wake times occur later, common in adolescents.

Polyphasic sleep A sleep pattern consisting of multiple sleep episodes within a 24-hour period.

Positive stress A manageable level of stress that helps build resilience and adaptation.

Prone sleeping Sleeping on the stomach, a known risk factor for sudden infant death syndrome (SIDS) in babies.

Prolactin   A hormone that supports lactation and has a calming effect, playing a role in sleep regulation.

Proprioceptive feedback   Sensory input from muscles and joints that helps the body to understand movement and positioning.

Quiet sleep   A deep sleep state in infants, similar to NREM sleep in adults, characterized by minimal movement and reduced responsiveness to external stimuli.

Rapid eye movement (REM) sleep   A sleep stage characterized by rapid eye movements, increased brain activity, and muscle atonia. This stage is critical for cognitive functions such as memory consolidation and emotional regulation.

Secure attachment   A classification of attachment associated with caregivers who consistently meet their infant's needs and provide reliable comfort and protection.

Sensorimotor stage   The first stage of the theory of cognitive development, spanning from birth to two years, in which infants learn about their world through their senses and actions.

Sensory processing   The way in which the nervous system receives, organizes, and responds to sensory input.

SIDS (sudden infant death syndrome)   The unexpected and unexplained death of a seemingly healthy infant, typically during sleep.

Sleep architecture   The structure and distribution of sleep cycles throughout the night, encompassing the stages of non-rapid eye movement (NREM) sleep and rapid eye movement (REM) sleep.

Sleep cycles   The patterns of transition between different stages of sleep throughout a typical sleep episode.

Sleep onset   The process of falling asleep, influenced by sleep pressure, circadian rhythm, and environmental factors.

Sleep pressure   Also known as homeostatic sleep drive, sleep pressure refers to the need for sleep that builds up during waking hours.

Synapses   The connections between neurons where signals are transmitted via neurotransmitters.

Synchronicity   The alignment of a baby's rhythms, such as sleep and feeding, with those of a caregiver to foster connection and regulation.

Vagal tone   Activity of the vagus nerve, the longest cranial nerve, which runs from the brainstem to the gut and other internal organs. It plays a key role in regulating autonomic functions such as heart rate, digestion, and the body's response to stress.

Vestibular feedback   Sensory input from the vestibular system in the inner ear that detects changes in head position, motion, and spatial orientation. It plays a key role in maintaining balance, coordinating movement, and influencing posture, motor control, and physiological regulation.

Disclaimer

The information provided in this book is for educational and informational purposes only and is not a substitute for professional medical, psychological, or healthcare advice.

If you have concerns about your baby's sleep, development, or well-being, please seek guidance from a qualified healthcare professional. Every child is unique, and what works for one family may not be the right fit for another.

The author, publisher, and Mother Nourish Nurture disclaim any and all liability for any direct, indirect, or consequential outcomes that may arise from the use or application of the information in this book. Any reliance on the information provided is at the reader's own judgment and responsibility.

Notes

Chapter 1

1. Ekirch, A. R. *At Day's Close: Night in Times Past.* W. W. Norton & Company, 2005.
2. Ibid.
3. Wehr, T. A. "In Short Photoperiods, Human Sleep is Biphasic." *Journal of Sleep Research*, vol. 1, 1992, pp. 103–107, https://doi .org/10.1111/j.1365-2869.1992.tb00019.x.

Chapter 2

4. Hirshkowitz, M. et al., "National Sleep Foundation's sleep time duration recommendations: methodology and results summary." *Sleep Health: Journal of the National Sleep Foundation*, vol. 1, no. 1, 2015, pp. 40–43, https://doi:10.1016/j.sleh.2014.12.010.

Chapter 3

5. Ionio, C., Ciuffo, G., Landoni, M. "Parent-infant skin-to-skin contact and stress regulation: a systematic review of the literature." *International Journal of Environmental Research and Public Health,* vol. 18, no. 9, 2021, p. 4695, https://doi.org/10.3390/ ijerph18094695; Field, T., Diego, M. "Vagal activity, early growth and emotional development." *Infant Behavior and Development,* vol. 31, no. 3, 2008, pp. 361–373, https://doi.org/10.1016/j.infbeh .2007.12.008.
6. Cregan, M. and Hartmann, P. "Computerized breast measurement from conception to weaning: clinical implications." *Journal of Human Lactation,* vol. 15, no. 2, 1999, pp. 89–96; Cox, D. B., et al. "Blood and milk prolactin and the rate of milk synthesis in women." *Experimental Physiology,* vol. 81, no. 6, 1996, pp. 1007–1020; Dewey, K. G. "Nutrition, growth, and complementary feeding of

the breastfed infant." *Pediatric Clinics of North America*, vol. 48, no. 1, pp. 2001, pp. 1007–1020; Daly, S. E., et al. "The short-term synthesis and infant-regulated removal of milk in lactating women." *Experimental Physiology*, vol. 78, no. 2, 1993, pp. 209–220.

7. Johnson, S. B., Blum, R. W., Giedd, J. N. "Adolescent maturity and the brain: the promise and pitfalls of neuroscience research in adolescent health policy." *Journal of Adolescent Health*, vol. 45, no. 3, 2009, pp. 216–221, https://doi.org/10.1016/j.jadohealth. 2009.05.016; Sowell, E. R., Thompson, P. M., Holmes, C. J., Jernigan, T. L., Toga, A. W. "In vivo evidence for post-adolescent brain maturation in frontal and striatal regions." *Nature Neuroscience*, vol. 2, no. 10, 1999, pp. 859–861, https://doi.org/ 10.1038/13154.

8. Henrich, J., Heine, S. J., Norenzayan, A. "The weirdest people in the world?" *Behavioral and Brain Sciences*, vol. 33, no. 2–3, 2010, pp. 61–83, https://doi.org/10.1017/S0140525X0999152X.

9. AAP. "Sleep-Related Infant Deaths: Updated 2022 Recommendations for Reducing Infant Deaths in the Sleep Environment." *Pediatrics*, 2022.

10. Baby Sleep Information Source. "SIDS and Safety." *Durham Infancy and Sleep Centre*, https://www.basisonline.org.uk/sids-and-safety/.

11. AAP. "Sleep-Related Infant Deaths: Updated 2022 Recommendations for Reducing Infant Deaths in the Sleep Environment." *Pediatrics*, 2022; Baby Sleep Information Source. "SIDS and Safety." *Durham Infancy and Sleep Centre*, https://www.basisonline .org.uk/sids-and-safety/; The Lullaby Trust. "Safer Sleep Advice." *The Lullaby Trust*, https://www.lullabytrust.org.uk/safer-sleep-advice/; McKenna, J. J. and McDade, T. "Why babies should never sleep alone: a review of the co-sleeping controversy in relation to SIDS, bedsharing, and breastfeeding." *Pediatric Respiratory Reviews*, vol. 6, no. 2, 2005, pp. 134–152; Wiessinger, D., West, D., Smith, L. J., Pitman, T. *Sweet Sleep: Nighttime and Naptime Strategies for the Breastfeeding Family*. Ballantine Books, 2014; Ball, H. "Parent-infant bed-sharing behavior: effects of feeding type and presence of father." *Human Nature*, vol. 17, 2006, pp. 301–318; Pemberton, D. "Breastfeeding, co-sleeping and the prevention of SIDS." *British Journal of Midwifery*, vol. 13,

no. 1, 2005, pp. 12–18; McKenna, J., Loughlin, J., Carrol, J., Marcus, C. "Cultural influences on infant and childhood sleep biology and the science that studies it: toward a more inclusive paradigm." *Sleep and Breathing in Children: A Developmental Approach*, 2000, pp. 199–230.

Chapter 4

12. Mohawk, J. A., et al. "Central and peripheral circadian clocks in mammals." *Annual Review of Neuroscience*, vol. 35, no. 1, 2012, pp. 445–462.

13. Sheldon, S. H., et al. *Principles and Practice of Pediatric Sleep Medicine*. Elsevier, 2005.

14. Davis, K. F., et al. "Sleep in infants and young children: part one: normal sleep." *Journal of Pediatric Health Care*, vol. 18, no. 2, 2004, pp. 65–71.

15. Chen, H., et al. "Rapid eye movement sleep during early life: a comprehensive narrative review." *International Journal of Environmental Research and Public Health*, vol. 19, no. 20, 2022, p. 13101.

16. Mosko, S. "Maternal proximity and infant CO_2 environment during bedsharing and possible implications for SIDS research." *American Journal of Physical Anthropology*, vol. 103, no. 3, 1997, pp. 315–328.

17. Hauck, F. R., et al. "Sleep environment and the risk of sudden infant death syndrome in an urban population: the Chicago Infant Mortality Study." *Pediatrics*, vol. 111, no. 5 pt. 2, 2003, pp. 1207–1214; Carpenter, R. G., et al. "Sudden unexplained infant death in 20 regions in Europe: case control study." *The Lancet*, vol. 363, no. 9404, 2004, pp. 185–191; AAP. "Sleep-related infant deaths: updated 2022 recommendations for reducing infant deaths in the sleep environment." *Pediatrics*, vol. 150, no. 1, 2022.

18. Moore, T. and Ucko, L. E. "Night waking in early infancy." *Archives of Disease in Childhood*, vol. 32, 1957, pp. 333–342.

19. Henderson, J. M. T., et al. "Sleeping through the night: the consolidation of self-regulated sleep across the first year of life." *Pediatrics*, vol. 126, no. 5, 2010, pp. e1081–e1087.

20. Peigneux, P. and Smith, C. "Memory Processing in Relation to Sleep." *Principles and Practice of Sleep Medicine*, Sixth Edition, Elsevier, 2016.

21. Besedovsky, L., et al. "The sleep-immune crosstalk in health and disease." *Physiological Reviews*, vol. 99, no. 3, 2019, pp. 1325–1380; Irwin, M. R. and Opp, M. "Health: reciprocal regulation of sleep and innate immunity." *Neuropsychopharmacology*, vol. 42, no. 1, 2017, pp. 129–155.

22. Irwin, M. R., et al. "Sleep disturbance, sleep duration, and inflammation: a systematic review and meta-analysis of cohort studies and experimental sleep deprivation." *Biological Psychiatry*, vol. 80, no. 1, 2016, pp. 40–52; Besedovsky, L., et al. "Sleep and immune function." *Pflügers Archiv - European Journal of Physiology*, vol. 463, no. 1, 2012, pp. 121–137.

23. Brown, A. and Harries, V. "Infant sleep and night feeding patterns during later infancy: association with breastfeeding frequency, daytime complementary food intake, and infant weight." *Breastfeeding Medicine*, vol. 10, no. 5, 2015, pp. 246–252, https://doi.org/10.1089/bfm.2014.0153.

24. Häusler, S., et al. "Melatonin in human breast milk and its potential role in circadian entrainment: a nod toward chrononutrition?" *Nutrients*, vol. 16, no. 10, 2024, p. 1422, https://doi.org/10.3390/nu16101422.

25. Brown, A. and V. Harries. "Infant sleep and night feeding patterns during later infancy: association with breastfeeding frequency, daytime complementary food intake, and infant weight." *Breastfeeding Medicine*, vol. 10, no. 5, 2015, pp. 246–252, https://doi.org/10.1089/bfm.2014.0153.

26. World Health Organization. *WHO Guideline for Complementary Feeding of Infants and Young Children 6–23 Months of Age*. WHO, 2023.

27. American Academy of Pediatrics. *Starting Solid Foods*. AAP, 2019.

28. Herbert, L. *Weaning Gently*. Mother Nourish Nurture, 2021.

Chapter 5

29. Kleitman, N. and Engelmann, T. G. "Sleep characteristics of infants." *Journal of Applied Physiology*, vol. 6, no. 5, 1953, pp. 269–282, https://doi.org/10.1152/jappl.1953.6.5.269; Sheldon, S. H.

Development of Sleep in Infants and Children. Principles and Practice of Pediatric Sleep Medicine, Second Edition, Elsevier, 2012, pp. 17–23.

30. Wong, S. D., et al. "Development of the circadian system in early life: maternal and environmental factors." *Journal of Physiology Anthropology,* vol. 41, no. 1, 2022, p. 22, https://doi.org/10.1186/s40101-022-00294-0.

31. Holt, L. E. *The Care and Feeding of Children: A Catechism for the Use of Mothers and Children's Nurses.* D. Appleton and Company, 1894.

32. Holt, L. E. *The Care and Feeding of Children: A Catechism for the Use of Mothers and Children's Nurses,* Fourth Edition, D. Appleton and Company, 1907.

33. Watson, J. B. *Psychological Care of Infant and Child.* W.W. Norton & Co., 1928.

34. Ibid.

35. Ibid.

36. Ferber, R. *Solve Your Child's Sleep Problems.* Simon & Schuster, 1985.

37. Hirshkowitz, M., et al. "National sleep foundation's sleep time duration recommendations: methodology and results summary." *Sleep Health,* vol. 1, no. 1, 2015, pp. 40–43, https://doi.org/10.1016/j.sleh.2014.12.010.

38. Hoyniak, C., et al. "The family context of toddler sleep: routines, sleep environment, and emotional security induction in the hour before bedtime." *Behavioral Sleep Medicine,* vol. 19, no. 6, 2021, pp. 795–813.

Chapter 6

39. Spear, L. P. "Adolescent neurodevelopment." *Journal of Adolescent Health,* vol. 52, no. 2, 2013, pp. S7–S13, https://doi.org/10.1016/j.jadohealth.2012.05.006.

40. Anders, T. F. "Home-recorded sleep in 2- and 9-month-old infants." *Journal of the American Academy of Child Psychiatry,* vol. 17, no. 3, 1978, pp. 421–432.

41. Cambridge Dictionary. "Co." *Cambridge* Dictionary, https://dictionary.cambridge.org/dictionary/english/co.

42. Cambridge Dictionary. "Soothing." *Cambridge* Dictionary, https://dictionary.cambridge.org/dictionary/english/soothing.

Chapter 7

43. Cambridge Dictionary. "Clingy." *Cambridge* Dictionary, https://dictionary.cambridge.org/dictionary/english/clingy.

44. Cambridge Dictionary. "Cling." *Cambridge* Dictionary, https://dictionary.cambridge.org/dictionary/english/cling.

45. Piaget, J. *The Origins of Intelligence in Children.* International Universities Press, 1952.

46. Sroufe, L. A., et al. *The Development of the Person: The Minnesota Study of Risk and Adaptation from Birth to Adulthood.* Guilford Press, 2005.

Chapter 8

47. Baryła-Matejczuk, M., et al. *Supporting the Development of Highly Sensitive Children.* Innovation Press, 2021.

48. Wolf, M., van Doorn G. S., Weissing, F. J. "Evolutionary emergence of responsive and unresponsive personalities." *Proceedings of the National Academy of Sciences of the United States of America,* vol. 105, 2008, pp. 15825–15830, https://doi.org/10.1073/pnas.0805473105.

49. Aron, E. N. *The Highly Sensitive Person: How to Thrive When the World Overwhelms You.* Broadway Books, 2013.

50. Ibid.

51. Thomas, A. and Chess, S. *Temperament and Development.* Brunner/Mazel, 1977.

52. Ibid.; Hipson, W. E. and Séguin, D. G. "Goodness of fit between daycare teacher-child relationships, temperament, and prosocial behavior." *Early Child Development and Care,* vol. 186, no. 5, 2016, pp. 785–798; Saudino, K. J. "Behavioral genetics and child temperament." *Journal of Developmental & Behavioral Pediatrics,* vol. 26, 2005, pp. 214–223.

53. Acevedo, B., et al. "The functional highly sensitive brain: a review of the brain circuits underlying sensory processing sensitivity and seemingly related disorders." *Philosophical Transactions of the Royal Society of London. Series B, Biological Sciences,* vol. 373, 2018, p. 20170161.

54. Jorquera-Cabrera, S., et al. "Assessment of sensory processing characteristics in children between 3 and 11 years old: a systematic review." *Frontiers in Pediatrics,* vol. 5, 2017, p. 57.

55. Little, L. M., et al. "Classifying sensory profiles of children in the general population." *Child: Care, Health and Development*, vol. 43, no. 1, 2017, pp. 81–88.

56. Beijers, R., Riksen-Walraven, J. M., de Weerth, C. "Cortisol regulation in 12-month-old human infants: associations with the infants' early history of breastfeeding and co-sleeping." *Stress*, vol. 16, no. 3, 2012, pp. 267–277, https://doi.org/10.3109/10253890.2012.742057.

Chapter 9

57. Center on the Developing Child, Harvard University. *Brain Architecture*, 2017.

58. Lee, K. et al. "Parity and sleep patterns during and after pregnancy." *Obstetrics & Gynecology*, vol. 95, 2000, pp. 14–18.

59. Nishihara, K. and Horiuchi, S. "Changes in sleep patterns of young women from late pregnancy to postpartum: relationships to their infants' movements." *Perceptual and Motor Skills*, vol. 87, 1998, pp. 1043–1056.

60. Lee, K. and Zaffke, M. "Longitudinal changes in fatigue and energy during pregnancy and the postpartum period." *Journal of Obstetric, Gynecologic & Neonatal Nursing*, vol. 28, 1999, pp. 183–191.

61. Driver, H. and Shapiro, C., "A longitudinal study of sleep stages in young women during pregnancy and postpartum." *Sleep*, vol. 15, 1992, pp. 449–453.

62. Karacan, I. et al. "Some implications of the sleep patterns of pregnancy for postpartum emotional disturbances." *British Journal of Psychology*, vol. 115, 1969, pp. 929–935.

63. Feldman, R., "Parent-infant synchrony: biological foundations and developmental outcomes." *Current Directions in Psychological Science*, vol. 16, 2007, pp. 340–345.

64. Leclère, C. et al. "Why synchrony matters during mother-child interactions: a systematic review." *PLoS One*, vol. 9, 2014, p. e113571.

65. McKenna, J. et al. "Experimental studies of infant-parent co-sleeping: mutual physiological and behavioral influences and their relevance to SIDS (sudden infant death syndrome)." *Early Human Development*, vol. 38, 1994, pp. 187–201.

66. Kryger, M. *Principles and Practice of Sleep Medicine,* Sixth Edition, Elsevier, 2016.

67. Lee, K. and Zaffke, M. "Longitudinal changes in fatigue and energy during pregnancy and the postpartum period." *Journal of Obstetric, Gynecologic, & Neonatal Nursing,* vol. 28, 1999, pp. 183–191.

68. Corwin, E. and Arbour, M. "Postpartum fatigue and evidence-based interventions." *MCN The American Journal of Maternal/ Child Nursing,* vol. 32, 2007, pp. 215–220.

Chapter 10

69. Etherton, H., Blunden, S., Hauck, Y. "Discussion of extinction-based behavioral sleep interventions for young children and reasons why parents may find them difficult." *Journal of Clinical Sleep Medicine,* vol. 12, no. 11, 2016, pp. 1535–1543, https://doi.org/10.5664/jcsm.6284.

70. Owens, L. J., France, K. G., Wiggs, L. "Behavioural and cognitive-behavioural interventions for sleep disorders in infants and children: a review." *Sleep Medicine Reviews,* vol. 3, 1999, pp. 281–302, https://doi.org/10.1053/smrv.1999.0082.

71. Owens, J. A., Palermo, T. M., Rosen, C. L. "Overview of current management of sleep disturbances in children: II—Behavioral interventions." *Current Therapeutic Research,* vol. 63, 2002, pp. B38–B52.

72. Bax M. C. "Sleep disturbance in the young child." *British Medical Journal,* vol. 280, 1980, pp. 1177–1179, https://doi.org/0.1136/bmj.280.6224.1177.

73. Leeson, R., Barbour, J., Romaniuk, D., Warr, R. "Management of infant sleep problems in a residential unit." *Child: Care, Health and Development,* vol. 20, 1994, pp. 89–100, https://doi.org/10.1111/j.1365-2214.1994.tb00856.x

74. Rickert, V. I., Johnson, C. M. "Reducing nocturnal awakening and crying episodes in infants and young children: a comparison between scheduled awakenings and systematic ignoring." *Pediatrics,* vol. 81, 1988, pp. 203–212.

75. Seymour, F. W., Bayfield, G., Brock, P., During, M. "Management of night-waking in young children." *Australian and New Zealand Journal of Family Therapy,* vol. 4, 1983, pp. 217–223.

76. Tse, L. and Hall, W. "A qualitative study of parents' perceptions of a behavioural sleep intervention." *Child: Care, Health and Development*, vol. 34, 2008, pp. 162–172, https://doi.org/10.1111/j.1365-2214.1994.tb00856.x

77. Hiscock, H. and Wake, M. "Randomised controlled trial of behavioural infant sleep intervention to improve infant sleep and maternal mood." *British Medical Journal*, vol. 324, 2002, p. 1062, https://doi.org/10.1136/bmj.324.7345.1062.

78. Reid, M. J., Walter, A. L., O'Leary, S. G. "Treatment of young children's bedtime refusal and nighttime wakings: a comparison of "standard" and graduated ignoring procedures." *Research on Child and Adolescent Psychopathology*, vol. 27, 1999, pp. 5–16, https://doi.org/10.1023/a:1022606206076.

79. Baills, A. "Treatment of behavioural sleep problems: asking the parents." *Journal of Sleep Disorders: Treatment and Care*, vol. 2, no. 2, 2013, pp. 1–7.

80. Blunden, S., and Dawson, D. "Behavioural sleep interventions in infants: Plan B - combining models of responsiveness to increase parental choice." *Journal of Paediatrics and Child Health*, vol. 56, no. 5, 2020, pp. 675–679, https://doi.org/10.1111/jpc.14818.

81. Mesman, J., Minter, T., Angnged, A., Cissé, I. A., Salali, G. D., Migliano, A. B. "Universality without uniformity: a culturally inclusive approach to sensitive responsiveness in infant caregiving." *Child Development*, vol. 89, no. 3, 2018, pp. 837–850.

82. Middlemiss, W., Stevens, H., Ridgway, L., McDonald, S., Koussa, M. "Response-based sleep intervention: helping infants sleep without making them cry." *Early Human Development*, vol. 108, 2017, pp. 49–57.

83. Mihelic, M., Morawska, A., Filus, A. "Effects of early parenting interventions on parents and infants: a meta-analytic review." *Journal of Child and Family Studies*, vol. 26, no. 6, 2017, pp. 1507–1526.

84. Whittingham, K. and Douglas, P. "Optimizing parent–infant sleep from birth to 6 months: a new paradigm." *Infant Mental Health Journal*, vol. 35, no. 6, 2014, pp. 614–623.

85. Blunden, S., and Dawson, D. "Behavioural sleep interventions in infants: Plan B - Combining models of responsiveness to increase parental choice." *Journal of Paediatrics and Child Health*, vol. 56, no. 5, 2020, pp. 675–679, https://doi.org/10.1111/jpc.14818.

86. Sroufe, L. A., Egeland, B., Carlson, E., Collins, W. A. *"The Development of the Person: The Minnesota Study of Risk and Adaptation from Birth to Adulthood."* Guilford Press, 2005.

87. Teti, D., Kim, B., Mayer, G., Countermine, M. "Maternal emotional availability at bedtime predicts infant sleep quality." *Journal of Family Psychology,* vol. 24, no. 3, 2010, p. 307.

88. Mihelic, M., Morawska, A., Filus, A. "Effects of early parenting interventions on parents and infants: a meta-analytic review." *Journal of Child and Family Studies,* vol. 26, no. 6, 2017, pp. 1507–1526.

89. Middlemiss, W., Stevens, H., Ridgway, L., McDonald, S., Koussa, M. "Response-based sleep intervention: helping infants sleep without making them cry." *Early Human Development,* vol. 108, 2017, pp. 49–57.

90. Mihelic, M., Morawska, A., Filus, A. "Effects of early parenting interventions on parents and infants: a meta-analytic review." *Journal of Child and Family Studies,* vol. 26, no. 6, 2017, pp. 1507–1526.

91. Whittingham, K. and Douglas, P. "Optimizing parent–infant sleep from birth to 6 months: a new paradigm." *Infant Mental Health Journal,* vol. 35, no. 6, 2014, pp. 614–623.

92. Gilkerson, L., Burkhardt, T., Katch, L. E., Hans, S. L. "Increasing parenting self-efficacy: The Fussy Baby Network® intervention." *Infant Mental Health Journal,* vol. 41, no. 2, 2020, pp. 232–245, https://doi.org/10.1002/imhj.21836.

93. Watson, J. B. *Psychological Care of Infant and Child.* W. W. Norton & Co, 1928.

94. Maute, M. and Perren, S. "Ignoring children's bedtime crying: the power of Western-oriented beliefs." *Infant Mental Health Journal,* vol. 39, no. 2, 2018, pp. 220–230, https://doi.org/10.1002/imhj.21700; Etherton, H., Blunden, S., Hauck, Y. "Discussion of extinction-based behavioral sleep interventions for young children and reasons why parents may find them difficult." *Journal of Clinical Sleep Medicine,* vol. 12, no. 11, 2016, pp. 1535–1543, https://doi.org/10.5664/jcsm.6284.

95. Mindell, J. A. et al. "Cross-cultural differences in infant and toddler sleep." *Sleep Medicine,* vol. 11, 2010, pp. 274–280.

96. Jenni, O. G. and O'Connor, B. B. "Children's sleep: an interplay between culture and biology." *Pediatrics*, vol. 115, 2005, pp. 204–216.

97. Fraiberg, S., Adelson, E., Shapiro, V. "Ghosts in the nursery: a psychoanalytic approach to the problems of impaired infant-mother relationships." *Journal of the American Academy of Child Psychiatry*, vol. 14, 1975, pp. 387–421.

98. Lieberman, A. F., Padrón, E., Van Horn, P., Harris, W. W. "Angels in the nursery: the intergenerational transmission of benevolent parental influences." *Infant Mental Health Journal*, vol. 26, 2005, pp. 504–520.

99. Guardino, C. M. and Dunkel Schetter, C. "Coping during pregnancy: a systematic review and recommendations." *Health Psychology Review*, vol. 8, 2014, pp. 70–94.

100. Teti, D., Kim, B, Mayer, G., Countermine, M. "Maternal emotional availability at bedtime predicts infant sleep quality." *Journal of Family Psychology*, vol. 24, no. 3, 2010, p. 307.

101. Middlemiss, W., Stevens, H., Ridgway, L., McDonald, S., Koussa, M. "Response-based sleep intervention: helping infants sleep without making them cry." *Early Human Development*, vol. 108, 2017, pp. 49–57.

102. Middlemiss, W., Stevens, H., Ridgway, L., McDonald, S., Koussa, M. "Response-based sleep intervention: helping infants sleep without making them cry." *Early Human Development*, vol. 108, 2017, pp. 49–57.

Chapter 11

103. Heraghty, J. L., et al. "The physiology of sleep in infants." *Archives of Disease in Childhood*, vol. 93, 2008, pp. 982–985.

Index